ROYAL
BARGEMASTERS

HM the Queen hosting a family tea party on board *Gloriana* at Windsor Park, 2013. (Picture by kind permission of Malcolm Knight Gloriana Trust)

ROYAL
BARGEMASTERS

800 YEARS AT THE
PROW OF ROYAL HISTORY

ROBERT CROUCH MVO
& BERYL PENDLEY LL.B

The
History
Press

Front cover: Gloriana with HM Bargemaster and full crew delivering the Stela in the Tudor Pull, 2018. (Picture by kind permission of John Adams)
Back cover: J.A. Messenger, with R. Turk on the right and W. Biffin on the left. (Picture from the Turk family collection)

First published 2019

The History Press
97 St George's Place
Cheltenham, GL50 3QB
www.thehistorypress.co.uk

British Library Cataloguing in Publication Data.
A catalogue record for this book is available from the British Library.

ISBN 978 0 7509 9083 7

Typesetting and origination by The History Press
Printed and bound in Great Britain by TJ International Ltd.

CONTENTS

DEDICATION

The authors wish to dedicate this book to Her Majesty Queen Elizabeth II in recognition of her rejuvenation and enrichment of the role of Her Bargemasters and Watermen during her long reign.

Since her ascension to the throne in 1952 and her first use of the Royal Barge to visit Greenwich in 1953, through to the magnificent river pageants for her Silver, Golden and Diamond Jubilees, Her Majesty has used her Royal Bargemasters and Watermen on numerous occasions, both on the upper reaches and on the tidal reaches of the Thames.

During the many decades of neglect and misuse of London's river in Victorian times and the dark days of the World Wars, before Her Majesty came to power, the Thames became polluted and was used less and less to stage events. However, during her reign the river was brought back to life, and is now cleaner, with an abundance of fish returning to its waters. Since her coronation, our Queen has, through six successive Bargemasters, refreshed Royal use of London's natural showplace.

Her support, and that of the Duke of Edinburgh, has meant that untold numbers of people have benefited from using the river for sport, display and to witness spectacular events, meaning that all can once again appreciate the importance of London's great natural asset: the Thames.

HM Bargemaster's plastron worn back and front of uniform. (Picture by Reflections Photography, with permission of Buckingham Palace)

FOREWORD
BY HRH EARL OF WESSEX

Some years ago, I had the privilege of experiencing what it was like to be rowed on the River Thames by the Royal Watermen. On that occasion we used the Royal Shallop *Lady Mayoress*, a 40ft shallow drafted rowing boat with a crew of seven, typical of the sort of vessel the gentry would use. It was a hint of days gone by when the Thames was the main thoroughfare through London and taxis were rowing boats called wherries, hailed by calling 'Oars!'

Britain has had a monarchy for over 1,000 years and for most of that time Royal Bargemasters and Watermen have been responsible for ferrying our Kings and Queens up and down the River Thames as well as protecting them. The river was by far the safest and most efficient means of travel and it's no coincidence that most of the Royal Palaces and Residences were built on the banks.

The story of the Royal Bargemasters and their long association with the Crown is as much about the Thames as it is about their Royal passengers. Huge congratulations must go to Robert Couch for embarking upon this personal journey to discover more about his predecessors in the role, and grateful thanks to Beryl Pendley for undertaking so much of the research. The result is a brilliant insight into a unique piece of history. Sadly Mrs Pendley died of a sudden illness before this book was published.

As with our monarchy, it's not just about the past. A couple of years ago I experienced the latest Royal Row-Barge, *Gloriana*, a far cry from the Royal Shallop. This magnificent vessel requires eighteen very fit oarsmen and a very proficient helmsman. It's a wonderful way to travel, but you do need to provide a little notice of your intention!

This book also recommends itself as groundwork for any future research into this fascinating subject and helps to fill one of the gaps in the wonderful and colourful history of our country.

HRH Earl of Wessex, KG, GCVO
30 March 2019

AUTHOR'S NOTE

By R.G. Crouch MVO

After serving over twenty years in the Royal Household, eight as a Royal Waterman and twelve as Her Majesty's Bargemaster, I became intrigued at how little had been written about the origin of these unique ancient appointments, which are so cherished within the Thames community. The more I searched back into the history, the more I realised how little had been recorded. Then during my time as temporary Clerk to the Watermen's Guild, I discovered a short piece in the Henry Humpherus *Watermen's History* that encouraged my obsession and triggered a determination to fill this gap in the history and origins of Royal Bargemasters and Watermen. The Humpherus entry is as follows:

The disputes between King John (who was then at Windsor) and his Barons, led to a conference to consider their grievances, being appointed. It took place on the 15th of June, at Runnemeade, (anciently called Running Meade) on the banks of the Thames, between Staines and Windsor, a place which has ever since been celebrated on account of this great event. The island by the upper end of it bears the name of. Magna Charta. Many of the barons and their followers proceeded to the spot appointed, in their barges and boats, and the two parties encamped apart like open enemies, (the country between Staines and Windsor was white with the tents of the ironclad men, who had come to demand a charte : of liberties) and after a debate of a few days, the King on the 19th of June, signed and sealed the Deed of Magna Charta, which was required of him. This famous deed, containing forty-nine clauses, either granted or secured very important liberties and privileges to every order of men in the kingdom, and clause twenty-three may be mentioned as providing that all kydells [fish weirs] for the future shall be quite removed out of the Thames and Medway. On the meeting breaking up, notice of the completion of the charter by the King was received with much enthusiasm by the assembled multitudes. The river was blocked up with the splendid barges of the nobility and others, the owners thereof getting away as fast as the embarkation could be effected.

Henry Humpherus, Book One, 1215

I now felt that I had a starting date of at least 1215 when the nobility were using the river in lavishly appointed barges.

My research being limited to the records at Watermen's Hall and the City's Guild Hall library, it was suggested by the Privy Purse Office at Buckingham Palace that I should contact the archivists at Windsor. However, on contacting them I was told that their records on the subject were at best ambiguous and only went back in any detail to the Victorian era. Everyone I spoke with agreed that the story went much further back in time and that it needed to be expertly investigated. I soon realised that I was out of my depth and needed help from a professional researcher.

Like all worthy stories, it was a piece of good fortune that changed my luck. Some years earlier I had reason to go to the College of Arms, which led to a meeting with Mrs Beryl Pendley, who was Assistant to Rouge Croix Pursuivant of Arms and was also taking her Bar Finals. She was very interested in the fact that I was involved with the Royal Watermen and we struck up an ongoing friendship.

We kept in touch intermittently and in later years I found that Mrs Pendley was now a professional ancestral researcher and had sustained her interest in the Royal Watermen. Upon hearing of my predicament, she offered to help with some appropriate research. The outcome was an agreement to work together on producing an authoritative book on the origins and progress of Royal Bargemasters. The subject has proved to be so intriguing that we have had to discipline ourselves to using research concerning only Royal Bargemasters and not be tempted into the many seductive offshoots of this subject.

There followed many years of difficult and time-consuming examination of the records at the various centres of archives in and around London to produce the raw data, which then had to be analysed and written up into a readable format. This book is the outcome of Mrs Pendley's work and our joint authorship, which we hope will be informative and which may prove useful to future writers on this subject matter.

For myself, it is a great relief to have achieved one of the aims of my river career by recording a first history of this obscure yet loyal group of men.

Robert George Crouch MVO

OBITUARY TRIBUTE

It is with great sadness that I report the death of my co-author Beryl Pendley who died of a sudden illness in early March 2019 while this book was being prepared for publication. Beryl was the person who persuaded me to continue with this book when I became overwhelmed by the amount of research required, who then joined me and used her skills as a professional researcher to seek out detailed information from the many obscure sources involved.

Beryl became fascinated with the book's subject matter and was rightly proud of her discoveries over the three years it took to complete her research. She was extremely determined and fastidious and kept us both on target by avoiding the many fascinating offshoots which we were tempted to follow up.

Although she was unable to see the finished product, she did see the various drafts and the final cover page image and was delighted when I was able to tell her that HRH Prince Edward Earl of Wessex had agreed to write a foreword to the book.

She will be sadly missed by her partner Eugene, her sons James and Royston and her beloved dogs. I will miss her as a mentor, friend and fellow author and I hope that her cheerful character will show through to the readers of this book.

Rest in peace merry Beryl.

Bob Crouch.

PREFACE

The reason for having a Royal Bargemaster and the Royal Watermen is to transport the monarch on water in a way that is fast, safe and comfortable, whilst at the same time offering an opportunity to display authority and majesty.

Over the centuries, the back-facing, seated mode of rowing was found to be the most efficient, but given the importance of the passenger, a particularly experienced waterman was needed to be facing forward to steer and pilot the vessel. This special waterman became the Royal Bargemaster.

As will be seen in the book, the Thames can be a difficult river to negotiate, made even more so in earlier centuries by Old London Bridge, which at certain tide times required great skill to negotiate safely.

Of course other methods of transport were available to the monarch – riding and carts or carriages. As we know, monarchs rode long distances throughout the country when necessary, especially where no rivers were available for water transport. Most of our monarchs were men, all of whom would have been experienced riders, trained to lead their armies into battle on horseback. Even Elizabeth I was a famously good rider.

Cart or carriage travel was very uncomfortable, at least until the arrival of sprung coaches in the eighteenth century. It was also very slow and relied on the roads being in reasonable condition, which was not always the case. However, it did afford the monarch some protection from the elements.

Both the above methods of equine transport presented security problems. Much of the country was a lot more wooded than it is today, offering opportunity for attack and robbery by ill-wishers and outlaws concealed among the trees. Thus any equine travel required a large retinue for protection.

This could not be avoided when the monarch needed to travel away from London, on 'progress' for example, where the whole court was on the move. However, the favoured transport option when the monarch wished to travel between their palaces in and around London was the row-barge. To travel by horse from Windsor to Greenwich could take days and was risky, whereas the same trip could be achieved in hours by row-barge, and was safer and more comfortable.

The Royal Bargemaster therefore became a very important member of the Royal Household, especially between the fourteenth and eighteenth centuries, so I was surprised when my early research revealed that these men had never been the subjects of a book. They have certainly been mentioned in numerous historical works, but 'always the bridesmaid, never the bride'.

After giving almost a millennium of royal service they deserved better, and thus this book was conceived. It is hoped that the book will demonstrate their importance to the royal families across the centuries and their relevance today. Even in these modern times, a beautifully decorated vessel on a back-drop of open water is still very impressive and can be used to great effect to display the majesty of monarchy, as our current Queen demonstrated so superbly during her jubilee celebrations.

Beryl Pendley

Contemporary river appointments still in use today. Front row left to right, Watermen's Company Bargemaster, HM Royal Waterman, HM Bargemaster and Fishmongers' Company Bargemaster. (Picture by Reflections Photography)

ACKNOWLEDGEMENTS

Photographic images by kind permission of: The Mansion House; The Canadian Maritime Museum; Dulwich College; Julian Calder, photographer; Christopher Dodd, author; Annamarie Phelps; Malcolm Knight, 'The Gloriana Trust'; Will Carnwath, 'The Gloriana Trust'; N. Crouch, Reflections Photography; S. Van den Bergh, Intaglio Print; Watermen's Co.; Vintners' Co.; Fishmongers' Co.; Richard Turk; W. Barry; HMB E. Hunt: MVO; HMB K. Dwan; HMB Paul Ludwig MVO; HMB C. Livett. Where not attributed, images are from public domain sources.

I

A BRIEF HISTORY OF THE ROYAL BARGEMASTERS

It is not known exactly when the first Royal Bargemaster was appointed. We tend to associate the Royal Barges, and thus the Royal Bargemasters, with the River Thames, but we need to remember that the early Norman kings spent a lot of time in France, their ancestral home and power base.

The Court was also very mobile in those days, and it may not have been practical to have a defined Royal Barge and an appointed Royal Bargemaster, either in England or France. It would have been more practical to hire vessels for transport when required. We have in fact found a reference to King Edgar the Peaceable being rowed in his barge by princes on the River Dee in 973 in order to show their allegiance, but with no mention of a Bargemaster.

The Anarchy of Stephen and Matilda from 1135–54 saw the rival monarchs constantly on the move, and thus the appointment of Royal Bargemasters may not have been uppermost in their minds.

Winchester, not London, had been the capital of the Anglo-Saxon kings and was also very important to the Normans, and to a lesser degree the Plantagenet monarchs. William Rufus was buried there in 1100, and in 1207 Henry III was born there.

Richard I spent only about six months in England during the whole of his reign, preferring to spend his time either in France or on crusade, where there would have been no need for a personal Royal Barge, and was completely absent for the last five years of his life.

It is thought that King John journeyed to Runneymede in his Royal Barge in order to assent to the Magna Carta in 1215. A number of the barons who attended as witnesses to the Great Charter are also believed to have attended in their own barges. Travelling by barge rather than by road when in the Thames Valley was just as important to the great noblemen of their time as it was to the monarch.

John's son Henry III was once caught up in a storm whilst in his barge on the Thames. The King was so frightened of the storm that he put in at the Bishop of Durham's palace, which was the nearest suitable landing place.[1]

Edward I frequently travelled by barge – payments were made to his bargemaster, Fulke le Coupere, in the summer of 1297 for taking the King from Gravesend to the bridge (a kind of jetty or causeway landing) at the Palace of Westminster. He was paid to wait at the bridge until the monarch was ready to go to Rotherhithe to visit the Queen of Navarre. From Rotherhithe, le Coupere took him to the hospital beside the Tower of London, and finally back to Westminster.

Richard II set out to meet the rebels by Royal Barge during the Peasants' Revolt in 1381.

Henry V spent much of his time in France, enough to require a Royal Barge to be sent there. On 18 June 1421, Robert Rolleston, Clerk of the King's great wardrobe, was paid £21 14s 8d to order and provide for the reparation, amendment and preparation of a certain 'row Barge of the said Lord the King, called *Esmond del Toure*, ordered to sail to France, to serve the said King in the river Seyne, or elsewhere, at the pleasure of the said King.'

Once the seat of the monarchy had been firmly established in London, the Royal Barge and thus its Master became more relevant to the day-to-day life of the monarch and the Court. Until the middle of the eighteenth century, London Bridge was the only bridge in existence in the capital, hence the reliance on travel by water.

Many factors have contributed to the role and significance of Royal Bargemaster over the centuries, including the state of the roads, the advent of modern horse-drawn carriages, new bridges being constructed over the Thames and which of the royal palaces became the primary residence of the monarchs. It should be remembered that the river was also used as a showplace, enabling the Royal Family to demonstrate their status with great waterborne pageants.

In Norman and medieval times, the roads in and around London were in very poor condition. After all, there had been no major road-building projects since the Romans left! Travel in the region was therefore slow, dirty and dangerous. Travel by Royal Barge was fast and comfortable by comparison. For example, a trip from Richmond to the Tower of London or Greenwich could be achieved in hours by water but could take days by road if conditions were difficult or the weather was bad.

Until Elizabethan times, taking journeys in wheeled transport was a less than pleasant affair. The vehicles were, at that time, slung on chains, so passengers were jolted around quite badly. This was improved somewhat by the introduction of carriages slung on heavy leather straps, and later by sprung coaches. It could also be dangerous in unsettled times.

Elizabeth I used her progresses (tours around her kingdom) as a political tool throughout her reign. In the early years of that reign she was trying to pursue a middle way in matters of religion, after succeeding her Catholic sister Mary. She needed to see and be seen, and to retain the goodwill of her people in these difficult times. Taking the Royal Barge along the Thames was the best and safest way to do this. To see and be seen in that delicate time, the Queen made two short barge trips on the Thames within a week in late April 1559. Flotillas of boats surrounded the Royal Barge, while Londoners lined the river banks to share in the music, water games and fireworks late into the night. The second celebration ended when gunpowder exploded, burning a pinnace and drowning one man. The river became a public stage that gave the Queen access to people and a smooth escape should circumstances dictate.

In Stuart times the ownership of a 'modern' carriage was also a great status symbol among the nobility and gentry. This eventually resulted in a proliferation of carriages for hire in the capital, to the annoyance of Charles II, who made a proclamation in 1660 to try to stem the use of hackney coaches.

Whilst these more comfortable carriages had a limited effect on the Royal Bargemaster and the Royal Watermen, it had a much more serious effect on the ordinary Thames watermen. The waterman and poet John Taylor (1578–1653) wrote:

Caroches, coaches, jades and Flanders mares
Do rob us of our shares, our wages and our fares;
Against the ground we stand and knock our heels
While all our profit runs away on wheels.

Another event which reduced the reliance of the monarch on water travel was the erecting of Westminster Bridge in 1750, followed by Blackfriars Bridge in 1769 and Battersea Bridge in 1773.

It was, however, the choice of the siting of their principal London residences that probably changed successive monarchs' day-to-day requirement for travel on the River Thames the most. This had a considerable impact on the importance of the Royal Bargemasters, causing their role to become less and less onerous over the centuries.

From Norman times until the late Stuart period, most of the royal palaces in London and the surrounding area were built on sites adjacent to the River Thames. These include Richmond, Windsor, Hampton Court, Bridewell, Westminster, Whitehall, Bayard's Castle, the Tower of London and Greenwich.

When Whitehall was destroyed by fire in 1698, St James's Palace became the principal London residence of William and Mary. Notably, it does not have river frontage. George I and George II also used this palace as their primary residence, but George III considered the old Tudor palace unsuitable for his large family and in 1762 purchased Buckingham House, later to become Buckingham Palace. Again, Buckingham Palace has no river frontage.

Of course, various monarchs continued to use palaces with river frontage, such as Hampton Court, Windsor, Greenwich and later Kew Palace, but this tended to be for pleasure or as retreats from central London.

More recent monarchs have relied almost exclusively on cars and helicopters to get around London and its environs, thus no longer needing to use State Barges on a regular basis. This has left the Royal Bargemasters of the twenty-first century with, generally speaking, a purely ceremonial role. However, in recent years they have also been part of the Diamond and Silver Jubilee celebrations, adding their colourful presence to these pageants and establishing that they still have a real part to play in royal events.

II

DEVELOPMENT OF THE ROLE OF THE ROYAL BARGEMASTER

The Royal Bargemasters and indeed the Royal Watermen would have been deemed as persons loyal to the Crown, due to the fact that they would be working in such close proximity to the monarch and other members of the Royal Family. They would be responsible for keeping the monarch safe whilst travelling on the river, along with anyone whom the monarch wished to use his/her barges, such as visiting royalty or foreign ambassadors.

As the following examples will demonstrate, the Royal Bargemasters and the Royal Watermen were present at some of the most important moments in our history as well as being very close to the monarchs as they went about their daily business.

General Travel by the Monarch and Royal Family

Prior to his investiture on 27 February 1490, Prince Arthur was rowed down the Thames in the Royal Barge. He was greeted at Chelsea by the Lord Mayor of London and at Lambeth by the Spanish Ambassador.

Lady Margaret Beaufort, the mother of Henry VII, made frequent trips by barge from her London residence, Coldharbour, to Richmond, where her son lay dying in 1509.

Henry VIII sometimes used the Royal Barge purely for pleasure. In 1539, he boarded his Royal Barge at Whitehall and was rowed to Lambeth. After evensong, he continued being rowed up and down the Thames, with music playing all the while.[1] When Henry was courting Katherine Howard in 1540, he was often seen being rowed to Lambeth of an evening to visit her.[2]

He also used his barges for pageantry. On 19 March 1541, he used the river to introduce his new Queen, Katherine Howard, to London. It was her first visit to the city as Queen. The Mayor and Livery Companies waited in their decorated barges between London Bridge and the Tower. One can only assume the tide was favourable, as the Royal Barge in which the King and Queen were travelling 'shot the bridge'.[3]

When Mary I of England arrived in London with her husband Philip of Spain on 18 August 1554, they travelled by water from Richmond, landing at the Bishop of Winchester's palace.

Elizabeth I used the Thames a great deal. In 1557, when she was still the Princess Elizabeth, she went from Somerset Place to Richmond to visit her half-sister Mary. She was taken in the Queen's barge, which was 'covered with a canopy of green sarsenet, wrought with branches of eglantine on embroidery, and powdered with blossoms of gold'.[4] On 10 June 1561, Elizabeth I proceeded from Westminster to the Tower in the royal barges to visit the Mint, where she coined certain pieces of gold, and gave them away to those about her.[5]

As we have said earlier, the Royal Bargemaster and the Royal Watermen were responsible for the safety of the monarch when he/she travelled on the Thames. During Elizabeth's reign there were various plots to assassinate her, as well as numerous rumours of such plots. On 17 July 1579, a shot was fired, injuring one of the Royal Watermen, as Elizabeth was travelling in her barge between Greenwich and Deptford. This was originally thought to be an assassination attempt, but on investigation turned out to be an accident.

On 17 July 1579, the Queen was in her 'privie barge' on the Thames between Greenwich and Deptford, accompanied by the French Ambassador; the Earl of Lincoln; and her Vice-Chamberlain, Sir Christopher Hatton. According to a pamphlet of the time:

[I]t chaunced that one Thomas Appletree a yong man and servant to M Henrie Carie, with ii or iii children of her Majesties Chappel, and one other named Barnard Acton, beinge in a boate on the Thames, rowing up and down betwixt the places aforenamed, the aforesaid Thomas Appeltree had a Caliver or Harquebush, which he had three or foure times, discharged with bullet, shooting at random verie rashly, who by great misfortune shot

This large, beautiful stained glass window depicting a rare image of Elizabeth I in her Royal Barge is positioned overlooking the great banqueting hall at the Mansion House in the City of London. (By help of Sir David Wotton and with permission of the Mansion House London)

one of the watermen (being the second man next unto the bales of the said Barge, labouring with his Oare, which sate within six foot of hir highnesse) cleane through both of his armes; the blow was so great and grievous, that it moved him out of his place, and forced him to crie and scritche out piteously, supposing himself to be slaine, and saying he was shot through the body. The man bleedin abundantly, as though he had had a hundred daggers thrust into him, the Queenes Majesty shewed such noble courage as is most wonderfull to be hearde and spoken of, for beholding hym so maimed, and bleeding in suche sorte, she never bashed thereat, but shewed effectually a prudent and magnanimous heart, and most courteously comforting the poore man, she bad him be of good cheare, and sayd he should want nothing that might be for his ease, commanding him to be covered till such time as he came to the shore, til which time he lay bathing in his own bloud, which might have bene an occasion to have terrified the eies of the beholders. But such and so great was the courage and magnanimitie of our dread and soveraigne Ladie, that it never quailed.

Appletree was arrested, brought before the Privy Council and sentenced to death. He was sent to the Marshalsea prison, where he awaited his execution. On the appointed day, he was paraded through the city to a gibbet by the river. Appletree said, 'I never in my lyfe intended to hurt the Queenes most excellent Majesty.' Before the execution could take place, Sir Christopher Hatton arrived with a message announcing that the Queen had pardoned him. Later in the same month, a petition was presented to the Earl of Leicester by Thomas Appletree asking that he be freed from his imprisonment in the Marshalsea, to which he had been committed for shooting unadvisedly, to the danger of the Queen, but for which he had received Her Majesty's pardon.[6]

Marshalsea Prison in Southwark.

In 1588, when Elizabeth I went to Tilbury to review her troops and made her famous

Armada speech, she left St James's Palace on the Royal Barge on the morning of 8 August. Other barges carried Gentlemen Pensioners and the Yeomen of the Guard. She was met by Lord Leicester and Lord Grey at Tilbury. She reviewed the troops that day, and on the day following, returning to London on 10 August.[7]

When Charles II had regained his throne he was welcomed by the lawyers of the Inner Temple with a lavish banquet on 15 August 1661. The main guests were the King, four dukes (including the King's brother, the Duke of York), a number of earls and the Chief Justice of Common Pleas. The guests went by Royal Barge from Whitehall to Temple Stairs.[8]

On the second day of the Great Fire of London (Monday, 3 September 1666), King Charles went to view the fire. He, together with the Duke of York, travelled by barge from Whitehall. After disembarking, they watched the destruction of the Watermen's Hall from a rooftop.[9]

After the Monmouth Rebellion in 1685, when the Duke of Monmouth and his companions were caught in the West Country, they were brought to London. It was reported that, 'Monmouth, Gray and Jermayn were brought from Fox hall to White hall in ye King's Barges … from whence they were carried in ye barges to ye Tower and through Trayters gate.'[10]

Although in this book we have concentrated on the bargemasters and watermen of reigning monarchs, it is worth mentioning the use of royal barges by Catherine of Braganza. After the death of Charles II in 1685, Catherine remained in England, residing at Somerset House (previously Denmark House) until finally returning to Portugal in 1699. It is clear that she had her own Royal Bargemaster, Royal Watermen and barges. Her Master of the Barges was Joell George. She had a number of Royal Watermen, including Sackvil Ride, Edward Hatfield, Francis Charlton, John Bernard, Phillip Seawell and Royly George. I think it is worth noting in some detail some of Catherine's expenditure on river travel during the period from October 1689 until the end of August 1690. It serves to demonstrate how much emphasis members of the Royal Family placed on river travel during this period in history, which could be described as being towards the end of the heyday of royal river travel.

Her Bargemaster, Joell George, submitted a bill covering three occasions for bringing 'the Back stares things and the Paige of the Backstares from Hammersmith to Sumerset house with the 12 Oard Barge', £4 4s 0d; 'The same time ye 8 Oard barge brought downe ye Backstares things', £3 0s 0d;

'The same time fore pare of Oares brought downe ye Backstares things', £1 4s 0d. The bill was dated 4 November 1689, came to £8 0s 0d and was allowed.

Joell George submitted a bill for services to her from 5–15 May 1690 which breaks down as follows:

> 5 May – 'Waitted one the Queene with the 4 Oard boat to Hammersmith' with 'One Gealle waiting at Somersett house the same time'. 8 May – 'Waitted one the Queene with the 4 Oard boat to hamersmith'. 10 May – 'Waitted one the Queene at Somersett house'. 14 May – 'Waitted one the Queene with the 4 Oard boat att Somersett house'. 18 May – Waitted one the Queene with the 4 Oard boat to Hamersmith'. The total bill came to £7 8s 0d and was allowed.

He submitted a further bill for services to Catherine for June 1690 which breaks down as follows:

> 5 May – 'Waitted one the Queene with the 12 Oard bargs to Hamersmith'. 10 June – 'Waitted one the Queene with the 12 Oard bargs to Grenwegs'. 11 June – "Waitted one the Queene with the 4 Oard boat to hamersmith'. 14 June – 'Waitted one the Queene with the 4 Oard boat as high as Lambeth'. 16 June – 'Waitted one the Queene with the 4 Oard boat to hamersmith'. The same time the '8 Oard Bargs waited one the Queene att Somersett house'.

The total bill came to £14 9s 0d.[11]

In the same volume as Joell George's bills are four further bills submitted by Catherine's Royal Watermen. These are particularly intriguing as they are for four fishing trips she undertook from the beginning of August 1690.

The first of the bills was submitted by Sackvil Ride and Edward Hatfield, 'for waiting on her Majesty in the ffore Oard Boat to Carry her ma'tie a ffishing att Windsor being 14 days beginning the first of July and Ending the 14th att 10s p diem', and comes to £7 0s 0d.

The second was submitted by Francis Charlton and John Bernard, 'For Waiting on her Ma'tie the Queen Dowager in her Fore-Oard-Barge att Windsor to attend her Ma'tie a ffishing 14 dayes beginning the 15th of July and ending the 28th att 10s per diem, wch allowing 10s for their charges from London to Windsor and back again, is in all £7 10s 0d'.

The third was presented by Francis Charlton and Phillip Seawell, watermen, 'Ffor waiting on her Ma'tie the Queen Dowager in her ffore-Oard-Barge att Windsor to attend her Ma'tie a ffishing 14 dayes beginning the 29th day of July and ending the 11th of August att 10s p diem (allowing 5s for bearing Phillip Seawells charges from London to Windsor and back againe wch is in all £7 5s 0d').

The fourth bill was presented by Francis Charlton and Royly George, watermen, 'For waiting on her Ma'tie a ffishing 14 dayes beginning the 12th of August and ending the 25th att 10s p diem (allowing Royley George 5s for bearing his charges to Windsor and going back againe to London)', amounting to £7 5s 0d.

Given that Joell George was Catherine of Braganza's Bargemaster and one of his watermen was named Royley George, I wondered if they could be related. It is not unusual for these appointments to run in families, as we will see with the Warners and the Masons in following chapters.

Research shows that Joell George married Alice Reeley at St Mary's, Newington, on 5 April 1660. Several of their children were baptised at St Mary's, Lambeth, including a Reeley George on 19 December 1660. When Royley George submitted his bill for his services in 1690, he would have been 30 years old, so it seems probable that Joell George and Reeley/Royley George were father and son.

Queen Anne was frequently on the river in her barge. Mr Hill, her Bargemaster, is said to have attended her daily to receive his instructions.[12]

The Royal Family continued to use their barges for entertainment during the Georgian period. In August 1715, the Royal Family, including the King, went by barge from Whitehall to Limehouse. Later that day they made the return journey, when ships moored on the Thames suspended lanterns from their rigging in salute. Houses lining the banks also showed lights. Many boats filled with members of the public followed the Royal Barge.[13]

In 1717, the King took his barge with various guests from Whitehall to Chelsea. They were attended by one of the City barges packed with musicians, who played a piece of music by Handel –this is believed to have been the iconic *Water Music*.

A contemporary article on the Water Music Pageant reported that:

On Wednesday Evening the King took Water at Whitehall in an open barge and went up River towards Chelsea. Many other Barges with Persons of

Quality attended, and so great a Number of Boats, that the whole River in a manner was covered; a City Company's Barge was employed for the Musick, wherein were 50 instruments of all sorts, who played all the way from Lambeth the finest Symphonies composed express for this Occasion by Mr Handel; which his Majesty liked so well that he caused it to be plaid over three times in the going and returning.[14] On the sixth of May 1741 the King took water at Whitehall, about five o'clock in the morning, and was rowed in a twelve oared barge through the bridge to Gravesend, where he set sail for Holland, his Majesty was accompanied by several other barges, in which were a great many persons of quality; he was saluted by the Tower guns.[15]

In 1749, Frederick, Prince of Wales took his barge on a pleasure trip. His barge was decorated in the chinoiserie style, and the Royal Watermen and presumably the Royal Bargemaster wore similarly inspired uniforms.

In 1822, George IV, having visited Ireland and Hanover, determined on a similar visit to Scotland.

'[T]here were great preparations,' says Lord Eldon:

to make his embarkation and voyage down the river, one of the finest exhibitions ever seen on the surface of Old Father Thames. The river and its banks from London to Greenwich appeared in the highest state of animation, swarming with human life and gay with brilliant decorations. His Majesty embarked at Greenwich on the tenth of August, by the royal barge to the *Royal George*, and was accompanied by the Lord Mayor and other civic authorities in the city barge, towed by the *Royal Sovereign* steam yacht. Thousands of voices hailed him as he passed the various places. At Sheerness, the Lord Mayor and other authorities who had escorted His Majesty down the river, parted with the royal family and returned in their barge to London; on His Majesty's return to London on the first of September, he was received with the same rejoicings from the mouth of the river to Greenwich, the Lord Mayor, & c, in their state barge, towed by the *Eagle* steam yacht went out to meet the royal vessel, and preceded it to Greenwich, where he entered his barge and was rowed by sixteen watermen in scarlett liveries.[16]

When the New London Bridge was opened in August 1831 by William IV, it was a great ceremonial occasion with water travel playing a large part.

The Royal Family and their entourage travelled in a fleet of carriages from St James's Palace to Somerset House, arriving at 3 p.m. From there they went by Royal Barge to the new bridge. 'The King (with the Queen on his arm) descended the stairs with a firm step, declining the aid of the proffered arm of one of the Lords of his suite.' The royal party then embarked on their barges for the trip to the bridge.

The Trinity House barge led the way, followed by the Victuallers' official barge and then another barge carrying Lord Grey and the Cabinet ministers. Then came the three Royal Barges.

The first of the Royal Barges carried the King and Queen, the Duke and Duchess of Cumberland, the Duchess of Cambridge, the Duchess of Gloucester, the Duke of Sussex and Prince George of Cumberland and Cambridge. The second Royal Barge held the Lord Chamberlain and the lords and ladies in waiting, along with the principal officers of Their Majesties' Household, and the third carried Her Majesty's maids of honour and officers in attendance on their Majesties.

The barges travelled at a sedate pace so as to make a great spectacle, arriving at the new bridge at 4 p.m. The King then opened New London Bridge, arriving back at the Royal Barges at 6 p.m. for the return journey to Somerset House.[17]

It was reported that:

The last occasion on which Her Majesty [Queen Victoria] went by state upon the Thames was in 1849, when she opened the new Coal Exchange in the City. On that occasion she embarked and landed on her return at Whitehall Stairs, as her proud predecessor Elizabeth had often landed before her. Since that year we believe that the royal barge has been allowed to slumber in its dry dock, and the royal bargemaster and watermen have enjoyed a sinecure.[18]

The Prince of Wales (later Edward VII) performed his first public engagement on 30 October 1850, when he was just 7 years old. He was accompanied by his father and the Princess Royal, travelling by Royal Barge rowed by the Royal Watermen, presumably under the supervision of the Royal Bargemaster.[19]

After the First World War, it was felt that tribute should be paid for the wartime efforts of the Mercantile Marine. On 5 August 1919, a water-borne

Royal Thamesis, up-river shallop based on Royal Barge design, shown here at the Thames Traditional Boat Rally, 1998. (Picture by Sue Milton, photographer)

pageant, the Peace Procession, took place, with King George V, Queen Mary, Princess Mary, the Prince of Wales and Prince Albert attending.

The jewel of the event was undoubtedly the 230-year-old Royal Barge, or more properly a shallop, which, with its scarlet-painted oars, was described as, 'Brilliant in its scarlet and white paint with gold ornamentation … with the crew in their antique livery and the Royal Standard flying.' The Royal Barge was rowed by eight Royal Watermen and was under the charge of the Royal Bargemaster, W.G. East, MVO. Mr East had won the Doggett's Coat and Badge Race in 1887, became England's sculling champion in 1891 and was appointed a Royal Waterman in 1898 and Royal Bargemaster in 1906.

Crowds lined the Thames from Custom House to the Cadogan Steps to watch as the Royal Barge and the other boats passed along the river. The procession left Custom House at 4 p.m., led by police boats and coastal motorboats, to a background of cheering from both sides of the river. In order for the procession to pass unimpeded for the first part of its journey, the Pool of London had been cleared of shipping. Flag-bedecked torpedo boat destroyers and police boats were moored along the South Bank, and even the riverside cranes were similarly decorated.

The water-borne procession went on, the buildings on the river banks full of cheering crowds. The bridges and also the Houses of Parliament were deco-rated for the occasion. The Royal Barge was accompanied by the Admiralty Barge, together with steamboats, cutters and all manner of vessels in large num-bers. When the royal party embarked at Cadogan Pier, they were greeted by a twenty-one-gun salute. They then took their places in the Royal Pavilion.[20]

Whilst Elizabeth I slowly abandoned the Thames for official occasions and pageantry (it is thought she took part in no river pageants during her reign), Elizabeth II has revived the Thames as a backdrop for royal pageantry.

On 27 April 1937, Princess Elizabeth and her parents, King George VI and Queen Elizabeth, went to open the new National Maritime Museum at Greenwich. Instead of travelling by car, they embarked upon the MV *Nore* at Westminster Pier and went in procession, accompanied by four tor-pedo boats and a Port of London Authority launch. *The Times* published the following report:

The Thames has had little of pageantry in its recent history, and until yesterday there had not been since 1919 [this refers to the Peace Pageant mentioned above] anything in the nature of a Royal progress along

London's river. The people of London enjoyed the occasion. It was impressive rather than picturesque. Many people who looked on at yesterday's procession remembered the grand old Royal barge, with its long scarlet oars. It had given place to the severely practical barge of a modern navy. With the change there had gone a great deal of the picturesqueness of river pageantry, but the swift relentless machine that had come on the scene was impressive in its efficiency and wonderful movement ... The modern age of mechanical transport seemed to have intruded into the traditions of Thames pageantry unheralded and with startling suddenness.[21]

This was the then Princess Elizabeth's first official engagement. At the time it could not be foreseen how, as Queen Elizabeth II, Her Majesty would bring the more picturesque pageantry back to the royal river.

Transporting of Dignitaries

When members of foreign royal families, foreign dignitaries or ambassadors visited England, it was usual for the Royal Barge to be sent to collect them from their ship and take them to whichever palace the monarch was in at the time. The usual place for the dignitaries to embark on the Royal Barge was Gravesend. Sometimes they arrived at Gravesend by ship, but they also often arrived by ship at Dover and made their way to Gravesend by road. Other barges were provided from the royal fleet to carry the entourages of the dignitaries.

Often the Lord Mayor and Sheriffs would escort the dignitaries in the State Barges belonging to the City, along with members of the livery companies in their barges:

To Walter Norman for his seventeen companions, lately remaining in the King's barge, as well by day as by night, upon the Thames, near the Sauvoye, for the safe custody of John, King of France, each of them receiving per day 3*d* for their wages. In money paid to them in discharge of their wages, – to wit, from the 2nd day of Sept last past, unto the 15th day of September then next following, for fourteen days, counting each day. By writ of privy seal amongst the mandates of Easter term last past £2 19*s* 6*d*.

Issue Roll, Michaelmas, 32 Edward III (1358)

In 1522, Charles V, Emperor of Germany, came to England to visit Henry VIII. He landed at Dover and made his way in a great cavalcade to Gravesend. They proceeded by barge to Greenwich Palace, where great public rejoicing took place when the two monarchs appeared in the Royal Barge on the Thames.[22]

When Cardinal Pole visited England on 23 November 1554 he was met at Gravesend. He entered the Royal Barge, on the prow of which was fixed his silver legatine cross surmounting a tall staff. He was then rowed to Whitehall, where he was greeted by King Philip and Queen Mary.[23]

In 1606, King Christian IV of Denmark, the brother of Queen Anne of Denmark, visited England. The Danish royal party arrived on 17 July. King James I left Greenwich with thirty-five barges to meet him. It is reported:

> King James's barge was built in the fashion of a tower or little castle, enclosed with glass windows and casements, faire carved and guilt, being wrought with much art, the roof being made with battlements, pinnacles, pyramids, and fine imagery, and upon this occasion it was towed by another barge with thirty oars.[24]

The barges continued to be used during the Interregnum:

> Warrants for payment were issued to Richard Nutt (i) warrant dated 20th September 1656 'for attending the Swedish Ambassador from London to Gravesend 15th Jan and bringing him back 17 Jan 1656 £17 10s 0d (ii) "for attending Ambassadors' £79 8s 0d (iii) 8th September 1658 'for fetching and carrying the Duc de Crepigny' £48 16s 0d and (iv) 28th April 1659 'for fetching up the Dutch Ambassador, October 1658 and attending Council to Somerset House' £8 0s 0d.[25]

During the Georgian period, dignitaries were still enjoying trips in the royal barges. For example, in 1733:

> [O]n the seventh of November, the Prince of Orange arrived at Greenwich, in the Fubb's yacht from Holland; he was met there by the Dutch Ambassador, and all the King's barges, who accompanied him in his journey to the Tower, where he landed, and proceeded to the Palace.

In 1763, two ambassadors extraordinary from the Republic of Venice arrived in England:

> The whole company assembled at Greenwich, from whence they set off between twelve and one o'clock; there were three state barges, viz., the Queen's of ten oars and two others of eight oars each, with another of six oars for their attendants, besides a great number of other barges, belonging to the nobility and gentry who accompanied the procession; they landed about three o'clock at the Tower, on their way through the City.[26]

We have examples of the transportation of dignitaries in the nineteenth century:

> [O]n Sunday July 14th HRH the Prince of Wales, attended by Captain Ellis, visited the Sultan of Turkey in the afternoon, and at 4 o'clock His Imperial Majesty and the Prince of Wales, attended by the great officers of His Imperial Majesty's suite, by the Earl of Bradford, Lord Chamberlain, and by Major General the Hon. A. Hood and Col. H. Ponsonby, Equerries in attendance upon His Imperial Majesty, drove in open carriages and four to Teddington, at which place the Queen's State Barges were waiting to convey the Sultan to Richmond, where His Imperial Majesty honoured the Duke and Duchess of Buccleugh with a visit to their villa on the banks of the Thames.

A few years later, in 1874:

> The State Barge built by Queen Anne in 1702, having been preserved at Windsor, was this year used for the conveyance of the Czar of Russia over Virginia Water. The rich gold work looked clear and brilliant, the plate glass windows shone in the sun, and she floated all smart with green and scarlett and gold, with her tarpaulin covering of red decorated with gold anchors, with her crimson fittings and gilt bead work.[27]

The last couple of examples were not really just about the transporting of dignitaries; they were about making an impression. Even in the twenty-first century, very important dignitaries such as heads of state are treated to the most impressive means of transport available to the monarchy. In a century where the monarchy has access to the finest limousines and helicopters, state visits involve the splendour of horse-and-carriage processions, which make a much greater spectacle and impression. They demonstrate the history and majesty of the monarchy in a way no modern transport can hope to.

Coronations

Until Charles II, the majority of monarchs travelled by Royal Barge to the Tower of London a day or two before their coronation, traditionally spending the night before their coronation there. On the day of their coronations they would travel in great state through the streets of London to Westminster Abbey to be crowned.

Henry V travelled from Kingston upon Thames to the Tower of London on 8 April 1413 and was met by 'a multitude of Princes, Earls, Barons, Knights, Esquires, and other great men of his kingdom, and likewise by the citizens of London, and an innumerable clergy'. 'On the following day he rode in procession through London to his Coronation, preceded by the Knights of the Bath, whom he had then newly created.'[28]

On 4 July 1483, Richard III proceeded to the Tower prior to his coronation, which took place on 6 July.[29]

When Elizabeth of York, consort of Henry VII, was crowned on 25 November 1487 she came by water from Greenwich to the Tower of London on 23 November. The following excerpt from *The Herald's Memoir* describes the scene:

And the Fryday next byfor Seint Kateryns day the queens good grace, royally apparelled and accompanyede with my lady the kynges modor and many other great estates, both lordez and ladyes richely bedene, came forwarde to the coronacion. And at ther commyng fourth from Grenewiche by water ther was attending upon her ther the maire, shriffes and aldermen of the citie, and dyvers and many worshipfull comeners chosen oute of every crafte in ther lyveres, in barges fresshely furnysshede with baners and stremers of silk, richely besen with the armes and bagges of ther craftes; and in especiall a barge called the 'bachelors barge', garnysshed and apparielede passing alother, wherein was ordeynede a great red dragon spowting flamys of fyer into Temmys.

The King had entered the City a few days earlier and was waiting to greet his Queen at the Tower of London. A similar red dragon was used at the coronation of Anne Boleyn in 1533.[30]

On 22 June 1509, Henry VIII and Queen Katherine travelled by Royal Barge from Greenwich to the Tower of London prior to their coronation.[31]

Edward Hall, the Tudor chronicler, described the first stage in the coronation of Anne Boleyn as follows:

> On Thursday 29 May, Lady Anne, marquess of Pembroke, was received as Queen of England by all the lords of England. And the mayor and aldermen, with all the guilds of the City of London, went to Greenwich in their barges after the best fashion, with also a barge of bachelors of the mayor's guild richly hung with cloth of gold with a great number to wait on her. And so all the lords with the mayor and all the guilds of London brought her by water from Greenwich to the Tower of London, and there the king's grace received her as she landed, then over a thousand guns were fired from the Tower, and others were fired at Limehouse, and on ships lying in the Thames.

Queen Jane was never crowned, but after her marriage to Henry VIII she and the King made a state entry into London on 7 June 1536 by Royal Barge from Greenwich to Westminster. They were followed by a barge carrying the King's bodyguard.

John Carter submitted his account for services on the eve of Edward VI's coronation in February 1547.[32]

Queen Mary followed the usual pattern:

> On Thursday, September 28th, Mary removed from St. James's to Whitehall, where she went on board her barge accompanied with the Lady Elizabeth, her sister, and other ladies and proceeded by water to the Tower, attended by the Lord Mayor and Aldermen, and all the companies in their barges, with streamers, and trumpets, and waits, shawmes and regals, together with great volley shots of guns, untl her Grace came to the Tower.[33]

Elizabeth I left Whitehall Palace for the Tower on 12 January 1559. The Italian diplomat, Il Schifanoya, describes it thus:

[H]er Majesty, accompanied by many knights, barons, ladies and by the whole Court, embarked in her barge, which was covered in its usual tapestries, both externally and internally and was towed by a long galley rowed by 40 men in their shirts, accompanied by a band of music, as was usual when The Queen goes by water.[34]

Charles I elected to travel to his coronation on 2 February 1626 from the Tower to Westminster by barge instead of processing through the city. Whether this was to avoid the risk of plague or he feared for his physical security is open to question. It may be that he regretted his decision, as his arrival at Westminster turned out to be somewhat undignified.

Sir Robert Cotton, a renowned collector of books and manuscripts, had hoped that the King would interrupt his river procession to land at Cotton House, his home beside the Thames close to Westminster, in order to collect a copy of the four evangelists on which he believed Kings of England had traditionally sworn their coronation oaths. Sir Robert's house and garden had been decorated and carpet laid for the royal visit. The King had other ideas and delivered an appalling snub to Sir Robert. He ordered that the Royal Barge should not land at Cotton House but proceed directly to Westminster. One of the witnesses to this event was Sir Simonds D'Ewes, who wrote, '[W]e saw the King's barge pass to the ordinary stairs where the landing was dirty and the incommodity was increased by the royal barge dashing into the ground and sticking fast.' The resultant clamber for the shore must have been very embarrassing for the monarch.

Charles II was the last monarch to process through the streets of the City from the Tower of London to Westminster on 22 April, the day prior to his coronation in 1661:

Upon the 23rd of April, being St. George's Day, about half an hour after seven in the morning the King entered into his rich barge, took water from the Privy Stairs, at Whitehall, and landed at the Parliament Stairs: from whence he proceeded up to the room behind the Lords' House, called the Prince's Lodgings, where, after he had resposed himself for a while, he was arrayed in his royal robes.

Elias Ashmole and Francis Sandford

So Charles II will have used the Royal Barge to travel to the Tower of London and then again on the day of his coronation.

When James II and his Queen, Mary of Modena, were crowned on 21 April 1685, they did not spend time at the Tower prior to the ceremony, but the Royal Barge still played a part on coronation day. According to Francis Sandford, Lancaster Herald:

> The night before, the King and Queen slept at the palace in St. James's. On the day of the Coronation the King passed through St. James's Park to Whitehall attended by several noblemen and officers of his household, going on board the royal barge at the privy stairs, he went privately by water to Westminster and about ten in the morning, landed at the Parliament Stairs, leading up to Old Palace yard; from thence he went directly to the Prince's Lodgings, and was there invested with his surcoat of crimson velvet.

Further celebrations included a water procession from Whitehall to Westminster on 22 April, followed by an aquatic firework display on the 23rd.

Once the tradition of spending a night or two at the Tower of London ceased, there was less participation in coronations by the Royal Bargemasters, but sometimes they took part in the processions. At Queen Victoria's coronation procession, behind the carriages carrying members of the royal family walked her bargemen and forty-eight Royal Watermen. Similarly, when King George VI was crowned in 1937, twelve Royal Watermen and the Royal Bargemaster took part in the procession.

State Opening of Parliament

Originally all of the royal regalia, which included the coronation and state regalia, was kept in the Jewel House at Westminster. However, there was a raid on the Jewel House in 1303, and at some point after it was decided that the bulk of the regalia would in future be kept at the Tower of London, whilst the coronation regalia was kept at Westminster Abbey.

Accounts show that building works were carried out at Richmond and Greenwich, and 'in the making of the Jewel house within the tower of London'.[35]

Prior to the state regalia being moved to the Tower of London, there would be no obvious reason for the Royal Bargemaster and the Royal Watermen to be involved in the State Opening, other than transporting the monarch to Westminster if he or she was residing elsewhere at the time. However, it would be necessary to transport the state regalia from the Tower to Westminster for the occasion, and this would have been safer and quicker by barge.

In 1531, John Johnson was paid £1 7s 4d for attending the King to and from Parliament with twenty-four men.

In 1536, after Henry VIII's marriage to Jane Seymour, he used the next State Opening of Parliament to introduce his new Queen to London. This State Opening began with a water procession from Greenwich. Events were organised along the route. Ambassador Chapuys organised one of them at Rotherhithe, which included a forty-gun salute. As the procession passed the Tower, another 400 guns were fired. The procession ended at York Place, from where the King rode to Westminster to open Parliament.[36]

The House of Lords Library records the three following events:

At the opening of Edward VI's first Parliament in 1547 the King withdrew to the privy chamber after the Lord Chancellor's oration and from there was escorted to the royal barge to be taken back to Whitehall Palace to wait until the Commons had elected their Speaker. After this time, monarchs quite often travelled to and from State Openings by barge, and thus derived the present role of the Royal Watermen in the ceremony ie riding on the State Coach to assist the Sovereign in alighting, passing the Crown to the Comptroller of the Lord Chamberlain's office on its arrival at the Palace of Westminster and assisting with the Sword if State.[37]

Sometimes, as at the opening of the Long Parliament on 3rd November 1640, the King proceeded to Parliament by barge to avoid the crowds and the danger of plague, when he was met at the Parliament steps by the Lords, judges and bishops and then processed with them through Westminster Hall and the Court of Requests to the Abbey.[38]

The ceremony of the State Opening lapsed after the opening of the Long Parliament by Charles I in 1640 and the abolition of the House of Lords in 1649. However, much of the ceremonial was revived for the opening of

Oliver Cromwell's 'other House' on 20th January 1658. Cromwell came by river from Whitehall to Westminster and thence by coach to the Palace in a magnificent procession, watched by a large crowd.[39]

On 15 August 1705, a Mr Warner, Master of Her Majesty's Barges, was paid £18 0s 0d for 'carrying goods to Windsor and for carrying the Crown to the Parliament House from 1704 Oct 24 to June 24 last'.

In 1714, Christopher Hill, Queen's Bargemaster, was paid £49 5s 0d for carrying the crown to the Parliament House and for carrying goods to Windsor, Hampton Court etc.[40]

In 1716, payment was made for sums due to the watermen and master of the barges for carrying the crown to the Parliament House and for attending the King, Prince and Princess.[41]

Although no longer responsible for transporting the state regalia from the Tower of London by river, the Royal Bargemasters still play a significant part in the ceremony to this day.

The Regalia of State is conveyed ahead of the Queen's procession from Buckingham Palace to Westminster. The regalia is taken to Westminster in

HM Bargemaster and Royal Waterman manning carriage on Dutch State Visit, 2018, one of the duties originally carried out by Royal Barge. (Picture by Reflections Photography)

what is called The Crown Procession. This consists of two carriages, the first carrying the crown, the sword of state and the cap of maintenance. The second carries the maces of state. Her Majesty's Royal Watermen proudly man these carriages in memory of their role of transporting the regalia by Royal Barge to Westminster.

On arrival at Westminster, the Royal Jeweller removes the crown from the first carriage plinth and presents it to the Bargemaster, who accepts it with due respect. He waits until the Palace Comptroller disembarks from the carriage, and then presents the crown to him on its travelling cushion. It is the Comptroller's duty to take the crown into the Palace of Westminster to be made ready for the Queen's arrival. The exceptional honour of holding the state crown bestowed on Her Majesty's Bargemaster indicates the historical importance of this appointment.

Royal Weddings

Royal weddings often involved river processions. After Prince Arthur married Katherine of Aragon at St Paul's Cathedral on 14 November 1501, there followed days of feasting and jousting at Westminster. This was followed by a great river procession from Westminster to Richmond.[42]

Henry VIII married Jane Seymour on 30 May 1536 at York Place/ Whitehall. According to a letter written by Sir John Russell:

> On Friday last [2 June] the Queen sat abroad as Queen, and was served by her own servants, who were sworn that same day. The King came in his great boat to Greenwich that day with his privy chamber, and the Queen and the ladies in the great barge.

On 4 June, Jane was proclaimed Queen at Greenwich:

> Three days later, the King and his new Queen, attended by the lords and followed by the guard in a great barge, went in triumph by water from Greenwich to Henry's new palace of Whitehall: vessels at anchor in the Thames fired their guns; the imperial ambassador greeted them with ordnance and music at Rotherhithe; the artillery of the Tower saluted them as they rowed past and music sounded as they shot London Bridge.[43]

Charles I and Henrietta Maria of France, having been married by proxy on 1 May 1625 in Paris, and in person on 13 June that year at Canterbury, travelled to Gravesend. There they were met by the Royal Barge for their journey into London. When they reached the Tower they were greeted by dozens of ships, which saluted by firing their cannons, followed by the firing of the Tower cannons.[44]

When Charles II married Catherine of Braganza in 1662, she, being a Catholic, could not have a Protestant coronation, so their marriage was celebrated by a magnificent water procession known as the Aqua Triumphalis. It did not take the usual route, but started at Hampton Court and ended at Whitehall. Although the procession did not take in the City of London, the Lord Mayor and the Livery Companies played their part in welcoming the new Queen. John Evelyn describes the Aqua Triumphalis as:

[T]he most magnificent triumph that ever floated on the Thames, considering the innumerable number of boates & Vessels, dressed and adorned with all imaginable Pomp: but above all the Thrones, Arches, Pageants & other representations, stately barges of the Lord Mayor & Companies, with various inventions, musique, and Peales of Ordnance both from vessels and shore.

He continues, 'His Majesty and the Queen came in an antique-shaped open vessel covered with a state or canopy of cloth of gold made in form of a cupola with high Corinthian pillars wreathed with flowers, festoons, and garlands.' Evelyn was involved himself, sailing amongst the pageant in his own vessel.

During the Georgian period, Royal Barges were still playing a part in royal weddings. On 25 April 1736, Princess Augusta of Saxe Gotha landed at Greenwich and was met by Frederick Prince of Wales. They dined together on the 26th, and he

gave her the diversion of passing on the water to the Tower and back in his barge, finely adorned, and preceded by a concert of music; the ships saluted them all the way, hanging out streamers ... They were married on the twenty-seventh of April; their son came to the throne as George the Third.[45]

Royal Funerals

On the death of Queen Ann, Richard III's consort, at Richmond, her body was conveyed to Westminster by water.[46]

Queen Elizabeth I also died at Richmond, and her body was taken by water to lie in state at Whitehall. Her coffin was placed on a black-draped barge in the dead of night and taken, with a flotilla of other torch-lit barges, to Whitehall.

On 22 June 1606, Sophia, fourth daughter of King James I, was born at Greenwich but she died the next day. On the following Thursday, her body was solemnly conveyed by barge covered with black cloth to the Chapel Royal at Westminster, where she was interred.[47]

The Queen Consort of James I, Anne of Denmark, died at Hampton Court on 2 March 1619. Her body was embalmed and placed in a lead coffin ready to be taken to Somerset House (sometimes called Denmark House) for her lying-in-state ceremony. A number of noblewomen and ladies had been commanded to go to Hampton Court to accompany the coffin on its journey by barge to Somerset House. Two heralds (Norroy and Richmond) were present, both to organise the noblewomen into strict order of precedence in the barges and to escort them all to Somerset House. The procession arrived at 8 p.m. that night.[48]

Administrative Duties

The Royal Bargemasters were responsible for payment made by the Crown to the Royal Watermen. We have evidence of this from two lawsuits brought against John Carter by widows of Watermen for withholding wages due to their husbands.

The Royal Bargemaster was also responsible for organising uniforms for himself and the Royal Watermen. At certain times the Royal Bargemaster took responsibility for organising tilts and furnishings for the barges. In 1508, John Thurston was paid for 'covering our barge and great boat in green and white cloth'.

In November 1529, money was paid to John Johnson for oars, 'paid to the maister of the barge for xvj Orys price of evy oer xviijd'.[49]

Chain of Command

During the reign of Charles II, the chain of command from the monarch to the Master of the Barges included Gentlemen Ushers. The following is taken from *Regulations for the Gentlemen Ushers in the Reign of Charles II*:

> Gentlemen Ushers' command of the Barge – It is the Gentlemen Ushers' duty to wait upon the King when he goeth by water, having power to command the King's watermen, which are sworne to obey him in the King's service; he also is to receive orders from my Lord Chamberlain, or from Mr Vice Chamberlains, and in their absence from the King, and according to those orders to command them what they are to doe. He hath also a place at the dore of the chamber of the King's barge to sitt att, which was then a great honour (and is so still) when noe man went into the chamber of the Barge, under the degree of lord or privy councellor, unless the King called them in, a second barge being ever appointed for all other gentlemen that waited upon the King as a second coach when he goeth by land.

Keeper of the Swans

It has long been assumed by river folk that the office of Keeper of the King's/Queen's Swans has been associated with the office of Master of the Barges, but generally it would seem this has not been the case. However, there is no smoke without fire, and a few of the Royal Watermen and Masters of the Barges have been involved with the royal swans in one capacity or another.

In the twelfth year of the reign of Richard II, Ralph Soot was appointed as Keeper of the King's Swans. He was not the Master of the Barges.[50]

In the sixteenth and seventeenth centuries, the post was often given to courtiers who already had royal appointments, as is evidenced by the following five appointments:

1 – 23 May 1509, George Assheby, Clerk of the Signet, to be, during pleasure, Master of the Swans in the Thames.
2 – June 1517, Ric Weston, Squire of the Body, became Master of the Swans.

3 – 10 May 1661, the office of Master of the King's Swans was granted to the Earl of Sandwich.

4 – 12 June 1672, the office of Keeper of the Swans was granted to Robert, Earl of Manchester.

5 – April 1683, the office of Master of All the King's Swans in the Thames and elsewhere was granted to Bernard Greville, Groom of the Bedchamber.

Noble earls hanging over the side of a row barge, trying to do a bit of swan wrangling, might not have been a very edifying sight, nor a productive one. It is quite likely that a Royal Waterman or Royal Bargemaster was paid to do the physical work with the swans. There is evidence to support this theory. In 1709, Isaac Crocker, one of Her Majesty's watermen, was paid £10 11*s* 8*d* 'for hire of men to preserve her Majesty's swans from the ice and otherwise this hard winter'. In 1717, a similar sum was paid to him for a similar purpose.[51]

Swan Uppers offering the loyal toast in Romney Lock. The post of HM Swan Marker was in the past sometimes held by the Royal Bargemaster. (Picture by Sue Milton, photographer)

The *Calendar of Treasury Books* for 1732 has the following entry: John Mason is to have the pension of £12 per annum, on Mr Stewart's establishment of pensions, lately held by Isaac Crocker, deceased, for the charge of going on swan hopping to mark the swans on the River Thames. In October the same year, John Mason is paid £12 for 'marking and nestling royal swans loco Isaac Crocker deceased'.[52]

When we reach the end of the eighteenth century and the nineteenth century, we do actually have Royal Bargemasters who held that office and the title of Keeper of the Swans concurrently. Richard Roberts was Keeper of the Swans in 1799. He resigned from both positions in 1808 in favour of his nephew, Thomas Alexander Roberts. John Roberts was then appointed as Royal Bargemaster and Keeper of the Swans in his place.

Today, the Royal Bargemaster is not connected to the role of Keeper of the Swans, now known as the Swan Marker. The catching of young swans is now carried out by the Royal Swan Uppers, the Vintners' Livery Company and the Dyers' Livery Company, while the care of the birds and their marking is under the control of a veterinary specialist.

There is an annual ceremony on the Thames in which cygnet swans are rounded up, caught, marked and then released. The Royal Swan Uppers wear the scarlet uniform of Her Majesty the Queen, and work from traditional rowing skiffs. It is accepted that these rowed vessels are the best suited for the work, as they are very manoeuvrable, relatively quiet and do not unduly disturb the swans. By royal privilege, the British monarch enjoys ownership of all unmarked mute swans in open water. Rights over swans may, however, be granted to a subject by the Crown. The only bodies still to exercise such rights are two Livery Companies of the City of London. Thus the ownership of swans in the Thames is shared equally among the Crown, the Vintners' Company and the Dyers' Company.

III

ROYAL BARGEMASTERS
SINCE EDWARD I

Compiling a list of the Royal Bargemasters proved to be more complex than had been expected. It is not always easy to tell whether a particular Bargemaster was appointed to serve the monarch or his/her consort.

Matters are further complicated when a Bargemaster is reappointed due to a change of monarch, especially where this occurs during the 'reign' of a dynasty such as those of the Warner, Mason and Hill families.

Yet another difficulty is trying to distinguish between the monarch's personal Bargemaster (the subject of this book) and those who were masters of his fleet of seagoing barges.

Further, where original documents have been transcribed (sometimes from Latin) and published, one is at the mercy of the people who indexed them. Sometimes Royal Bargemasters are indexed by name only, which if the name is unknown at the time of research, can be somewhat trying. Even when the name is known, spelling can vary, as prior to about 1750 spelling was not much thought about. They are often indexed by job title, but this has varied over the centuries – Bargemaster, Barge-Master, Master of the Barges, Maister of the Barges and even plain Bargeman. Sometimes they are grouped under headings such as the monarch's name, transport or even ships!

Given the above difficulties, it is possible that the odd Royal Bargemaster may have been left out or that a master of the monarch's seagoing barges may have been included by mistake.

The amount of information available for each Bargemaster varies due to the time in history when they served and their length of service. Some were in service for many years, but others served only for a couple of years.

We have included fairly lengthy pieces about the more recent Royal Bargemasters as we feel that we have a duty to include details of their background and their reminiscences about their time in office for future generations to have access to.

At the time of publication, no names could be found for Royal Bargemasters earlier than those shown on the following list.

THOMAS ELYOT

Master of the Barges to Edward I.

He appears in the 1285–86 accounts on several occasions, being paid for the transportation of the King and Queen and their family on journeys between the Tower of London and Fulham, also from Westminster to Gravesend. Summaries of his accounts for that period include the wages of the watermen, including on one occasion twelve men in a separate boat to pull/tow the Royal Barge.[1]

FULKE LE COUPERE

Master of the Barges to Edward I.

In 1299, Le Coupere and Absalom of Greenwich oversaw the movement of a flotilla of 115 barges carrying the King and his family and his effects up the Thames from Gravesend to Westminster.

ABSALOM OF GREENWICH

Master of the Barges to Edward II.

3 April 1292 (Westminster) – safe conduct for one year for Absalom le Mariner of Greenwich, going with a boat of R. Bishop of Bath and Wells, the chancellor, to diverse places along the Thames, on the bishop's and his own affairs.

WALTER FESALOCK/FESACOCK

Bargemaster to Richard II.

Granted the office of Gatekeeper of London Bridge by writ of Privy Seal in 1385. The writ describes him as 'one of his (the King's) bargemen'. He was to pay the King 13s 4d a year.

9 February 1392 (Westminster) Grant for life, to Walter Vesecock, master of the King's barge, for service to the late prince as well as to the King, and in consideration of his age and infirmity and of his never having had any remuneration, of 2*d* a day at the Exchequer.

ROBERT ATTE WERE

17 June 1400 – payment for half a year by bill of the Treasurer of the household.

WILLIAM GODEMAN

Master of the Barges to Henry IV.[2]
  Master of the Barges to Henry V.[3]
  William Godeman became Master of the Barges after the death of Robert atte Were *c*.1413.

JOHN CALCOTE/CALCOTT

Master of the Barges to Henry VI.
  He was sentenced to death for high treason on 23 August 1463 during the reign of Edward IV. In 1485, his son, also John, petitioned Henry VII for the return of his father's property, in which he succeeded – see below:

56. [61.] Item, another petition was presented to the same lord king in the aforesaid parliament by the commons of the realm of England being in the same parliament, on behalf of John Calcote, citizen and painter of London, son of John Calcote late of Lambeth, in these words:
  'To the most wise and discreet commons assembled in this present parliament; the king's true liegeman John Calcote, citizen and painter of London, son of John Calcote late of Lambeth and master of the barge of the most Christian prince King Henry VI, late king of England, most humbly shows to your great wisdoms that where the said John Calcote the father, by a false accusation made to King Edward IV, late king of England, was impeached of high treason, and afterwards, before commissioners of oyer and terminer sitting in Southwark on 23 August in the third year of the reign of the said King Edward IV [1463], was arraigned, and by great threats made to twelve men, was attainted and sentenced to death, as more

fully appears in the record of the same. On the strength of which attainder, all the lands and tenements and other possessions which belonged to the said John Calcote the father at the time of the said attainder were forfeited; and your said petitioner, who should have been the heir of his said father by common law or custom if the said attainder had not happened, and his heirs were disinherited and disabled by occasion of the same attainder. All of which things were done to the said John Calcote the father for his true heart and service which he did and owed to the said most Christian prince King Henry VI.

May it please your said wisdoms, in consideration of the foregoing, of your manifold charity and for *[memb. 39]* the love of God, to pray our sovereign lord the king, by the advice and assent of the lords spiritual and temporal assembled in this present parliament, and by authority of the same, to ordain and decree that the said attainder, with everything consequent upon it, and the record of it, as to the things stated and every part of them, be entirely void and of no effect against the said John Calcote the father and his heirs. And that your suppliant and his heirs may enter, have and inherit all the lands and tenements which belonged to the said John Calcote the father, as he should have done by common law or custom after the death of the said John the father if the said attainder had not been had or made. And that your said suppliant may enter upon the possession of our sovereign lord as well as upon the possession of any other person or persons into all such lands and tenements, and all other things of which the said John the father, or anyone else to his use, was seised at the time of the said attainder or of the supposed treason or at any time since, and to have and hold them, and each of them, as though the said attainder had never been had, made or done. And by the said authority be it ordained that no person be vexed or troubled by your said suppliant or any of his heirs, or feoffees to his use, for taking any issues and profits of such lands and tenements since the said attainder and before the first day of this present parliament, but should be entirely quit and discharged of the same; saving to all the king's lieges all such right, title and interest as they, or any of them, had in the things stated on the said 23 August or at any time since, other than by the letters patent of the said late King Edward IV, King Richard III, or by occasion of the said attainder. When this petition had been read, heard and fully understood in the aforesaid parliament, by the advice and assent of the lords spiritual and temporal likewise being in the said parliament, and at the request of the aforesaid commons, and by authority of the same, it was answered:

Let it be done as it is desired.'

ROBERT BIGGER/BRIGGER

Master of the Barges to Edward IV.[4]

No appointment date has been found. He seems to have been given the appointment possibly as a reward.

Edward IV – April 1463:

Provided also that this act of resumption or annulment shall not extend or be prejudicial in any way to Robert Brigger, by whatever name he is called, with regard to a grant made by us to him of 7*d* halfpenny a day, to be taken yearly from the issues, profits, farms and revenues of the county of Devon by the hands of the sheriff of the same county at the time, at Easter and Michaelmas in equal portions, from Michaelmas in the second year of our reign [1462] until the same Robert has an adequate office by our grant for term of his life of the value of 7*d* halfpenny a day or more: but that our aforesaid grant and letters patent shall be good and effectual in the law to the said Robert, according to the tenor and purport of the same letters patent, notwithstanding the said act (fn.v–496–965–1)

JOHN PHILIP

Master of the Barges to Edward IV.

ROBERT SAVAGE

Bargemaster to Henry VII.

Appointed 25 November 1486.

Grant, for life, to Robert Savage, of the office of master and keeper of the King's barge, with such wages as Robert Brigger had of the Grant of Edward IV, on surrender of a former patent 17 November 1485 granting the same office to him for life, with the usual wages. Given at Greenwich.

Humpheris states that in the Act of Resumption, passed in the first year of the reign of Henry VII, Robert Savage was protected in the grant of the office of master of the King's barge.

LEWIS WALTER (also known as LEWYS WALTIER)

Lewis Walter/Lewys Waltier was Bargemaster (or Bargeman) to Elizabeth of York, the wife of Henry VII.

There are numerous references to him contained within the Privy Purse Expenses of Elizabeth of York for 1502, including:

Item viij day of Apelle to Lewys Waltier bargeman for conveying the Quenes grace from Richmount to Greenwiche the ij of Aprille in hire barge with xxj rowers every rower taking viiij, the maister xvj d and the reward of a barge beneath the brigge xvj d [the 'reward' was for 'shooting the bridge'].

Item the ij day of May conveying the Quene from the Tower to Greenwiche with xxj rowers xiiij s [shillings] and to the maister xvj d [pence].

Item the sixth day of May conveying the Quene from Greenwiche to Richmounte with xxj rowers at viij d the rowers xiiij and the maister xvjd.

Item a grete boat the same day conveying the ladyes and gentilwomen from Greenwiche to Richmounte with ix rowers at viij d, the rowers vj s and tha maister xvj d.

In November 1502, Lewis was paid for conveying the Queen and her ladies from Richmond to Westminster; taking the princesses in the Queen's barge 'from the Bisshop of Duresme Place to Westminster'; and conveying the Queen and her ladies from Westminster to Greenwich; from Greenwich to Baynard's Castle and from Baynard's Castle to Westminster. The frequency of these journeys in just two months of 1502 show the great reliance that the Royal Family placed on travel by water and thus upon their Royal Bargemasters and Royal Watermen.

It is interesting to note that at this point in history, the office of Master of the Barges is also referred to simply as Bargeman.

JOHN WEST

John West was Bargemaster to Henry VII from July 1497 until 1501/02. On 3 December 1498, he was provided with a tilt for the great barge and ballinger, a carpet and a cushion.

JOHN THURSTONE/THRUSTON

Appointed 26 September 1509 'to be master of the King's barge, during pleasure'.[5]

Given that it was customary to reappoint Royal Bargemasters during the first year of the reign of the incoming monarch, the appointment dated 26 September 1509 was probably just such a case. Thus it is probable that John Thurstone was the successor to John West, who was Bargemaster from 1497 to 1502.

In 1513 he was involved in the movement of the King's Guard. A warrant was issued on 28 June to John Daunce to pay John Thurstone, master of the King's barge, £15 5s 4d 'for hire of barges and crayers to carry the Guard from Greenwich to Feversham by water'. Thurstone's receipt for the money is dated the same day.[6]

He was also involved with caring for the royal barges. In the Exchequer Accounts of 1514, a warrant was issued to the Great Wardrobe to deliver John Thurston, Master of the Barge, 'two tiltes, one for our barge and another for our boat'.[7]

Accounts of 1516 regarding fees and annuities record that John Thurston, Master of the Barge, received 7½d a day 'during pleasure'. Wages of twenty men for attending to the barge were 20s each a year.

Thurstone was naturally involved with the usual duties of the Master of the Barge, as is evidenced by his accounts submitted for payment on 12 July 1517:

> 29 June, 2, 4, 5, 7 and 8 July: for conveying the ambassadors of Burgoyne from the Tower to Greenwich and back again by order of Lord Aburgoyne and Sir Henry Marney.
>
> 30 June and 9 July: for conveying the same from the Crane in the Vyntre to the Cardinal's place.
>
> 11 and 12 July: for conveying the same from London to Gravesend

For the Ambassadors of France 7s 8d. Total £9 2s 4d of which sum John Thurston, the master, acknowledges the receipt from Sir John Daunce.

JOHN JOHNSON

Appointed August 1526: 'John Johnson, page of the Queen's Chamber. Grant, during pleasure of the office of the King's barge and boat, vice John Thurston.'[8]

In the period that John Johnson was Henry VIII's Bargemaster, as well as being involved in the King's day-to-day transport, he was probably witness to many events of historical note during those turbulent times.

He was Bargemaster when Henry was courting Anne Boleyn. In October 1529, Henry, accompanied by Anne and her mother, went to inspect work being carried out to York Place for Anne. On 2 November that year, the King left Greenwich to take up residence with Anne at York Place.

On 13 February 1531 – 'paid to John the king's bargeman, for coming twyes from Grenewiche to York Place with a great bote with books for the king xiijs iiijd.'

A warrant was given to John Johnson, master of the King's barge, for attending on the King to and from Parliament on 31 March Henry VIII with twenty-four men by the Lord Chamberlain's command.[9]

On 8 February 1533, Henry took the French Ambassador and the Papal Nuncio in the Royal Barge from Greenwich to Westminster for a ceremony in which the new Speaker was presented to him.

On 21 August that same year, the King and Queen Anne (by now heavily pregnant) left Windsor Castle for Greenwich by barge. They stopped for a few days at York Place, and on 26 August continued their journey by water to Greenwich, where Anne was to give birth to their daughter Elizabeth.

Anne Boleyn was beheaded on 15 May 1536. It is said that when Henry heard the news, he took to his barge to go immediately to Jane Seymour. Two days after Henry and Jane were married, they left York Place and went to Greenwich by barge.

On 7 June came the State Opening of Parliament, which began with a river procession from Greenwich to York Place. As the procession passed the Tower, bedecked with streamers, 400 shots were fired. The procession continued to London Bridge: 'So the King passed through London Bridge, with his trumpets blowing before him, and shawms and sackbuts and drumslades playing also in barges going before him.'[10]

The year 1540 was a busy time for John Johnson.

He would also have been present when, a few days after their marriage on 6 January 1540, Henry and his new wife, Anne of Cleves, left Greenwich. They moved by water to Whitehall in a great river pageant.

The expenses of Henry VIII for 1540 show three payments relating to the work of John and his watermen:

John Johnson, master of the King's barge, with 10 men, bringing the barge from Westminster to Greenwich, 3 Feb., himself at 16*d*, and the watermen at 8*d* a day, 8*s*; also with 25 watermen, 'carrying the Guard, in the said barge from Greenwich to Westminster' 4 Feb; also 'for iiij burdens of rushes for the said barge', viijd; on the Vice-Chamberlain's bill, total 26*s* 8*d*.

John Johnson, master of the King's barge, with 24 men, 'going with the great barge from Greenwich to Gravesend for the strange ambassador [the Duke of Ferrara's brother] and for the bringing of them from thence to London' 2 days, himself at 2*s* and men at 12*d* a day each, in the month of July; again 'giving attendance upon the said ambassador and bringing them from London to Westminster and to London again, from thence to Lambeth and to London and so to Westminster,' 4 days, in the said month of July; also 'for burning and tallowing the said barge, xs., and for rushes, ijs' again 'going to Greenwich with the said ambassador and to London again the xxvij day of July,' himself at 16*d* and men at 8*d*, and 'carrying the said ambassador from London to Gravesend and bringing up the barge again the xxix day of July,' himself at 2*s* and men at 12*d*; on the Vice-Chamberlain's bill, £4 2*s*.

John Johnson, master of the King's barge, with 24 men, 'serving the strangers [The Prince of Salerno and Don Luis d'Avila] in the great barge from London to Westminster and so to London again,' himself at 16*d* a day and his men at 8*d*; again serving them 3 days in July; 'and for rushes for the same barge xijd., also for brynnyng the said barge of the blocks and washing her, ijs' for 'another barge that brought the said strangers from Powles wharf to the Tower,' 12 July, wherein were 10 watermen and a steerer, each man at 8*d* and the steerer 16*d* a day, and for the hire of the said barge 12*d*; on the Vice-Chamberlain's bill.

John Johnson died later that year.

It is worth noting that Richard Molle was Master of the Queen's Barge during John Johnson's tenure as King's Bargemaster. In 1531, he was paid 17*s* 10*d* on the Lord Chamberlain's account, as Master of the Queen's Barge, for conveying the legate Campegius to Bridewell with twenty-four oars.[11]

JOHN CARTER

Appointed 6 November 1540 for life.

A payment was made in December 1531 to 'Carter one of the King's watermen in rewarde for dressing of the King's barge xxs', so he was still just a waterman at that date.

He may have been deputy to John Johnson, as in 1532 there was a payment to him 'for serving the King with the grete barge and xvij men to the Towre, twyes, xxs and vijd'.[12]

According to Letters and Papers F & D of Henry VIII Vol.16, 1540–41, John Carter was Master of the King's Barge: 'Grant for life of the office of the King's barge and boats which John Johnson, deceased lately held.'

He was involved in the coronation of Edward VI in February 1547.[13]

On 21 July 1548, John Carter was paid £6 2*s*, 'expended about His Majesty's Affaires, concerning the Barges'.

Two widows of Royal Watermen brought actions against John Carter for wages due to their husbands which he was withholding (National Archives). These were the widows of John Langton and John Davy.

THOMAS RAGGE

Appointed 20 January 1550.

> Grant for life to the King's servant, Thomass Ragge, master of the King's barge and 'le bootes' which John Carter, deceased had, with profits as enjoyed by the said Carter, John Johnson, John Thruston or any other occupant of that office, receiving his fees at the Receipt of the Exchequer from Christmas 3 EdVI.[14]

JOHN BOUNDY/BONDY/BUNDYE

'Warrant to the Treasurer of the Chamber to pay unto John Boundy, Master of the King's Barges £4 13*s* due for men's wages.'

In 1552, Boundy appears to have got himself into some kind of trouble. On 1 October, the Bailiff of Westminster was ordered to 'apprehend Bondy, Master of the King's Barge, and to bring him hither with diligence, and so as none speak with him untyll he be brought before the Lords'.

THOMAS COXE

Appointed 16 January 1554.

Grant for life to the queen's servant Thomas Coxe of the office of master of the Queen's barges and the boats, which office John Bundye deceased, lately held, with the wages and fees of the same to be received at the Receipt of the Exchequer. To hold the office as fully as Bundye or Thomas Ragge, John Carter, John Johnson, John Thruston or other persons.[15]

RICHARD DREWE

Appointed 10 November 1558.

Grant for life in consideration of his service, to Richard Drewe of the place and office of master of the King and Queen's barge and boats which Thomas Coxe, deceased, lately held, with all such wages and profits of the office as Coxe, John Bundy, Thomas Ragge, John Carter, John Johnson or John Thruston had, to be paid at the usual feasts at the Receipt of the Exchequer from midsummer day last; notwithstanding that mention is not made in the presents of the true valuation of the premises.[16]

WILLIAM SCARLETT

Master of the Barges to Elizabeth I.
He is the defendant in the Chancery Proceeding Ireland v Scarlett.[17]

WILLIAM DORRETT

A 1593 Petition was signed by William Dowet, Master of HM Barges.
William Dorrett was described as Master of Her Majesty's Barges when he was appointed as one of the overseers of the will of Thomas Moore,

waterman, in 1598. Dorrett was granted livery for himself and thirty-six watermen for the funeral of Elizabeth I in 1603. One of the watermen was Richard Warner – see below.[18]

RICHARD WARNER Snr

Appointed jointly with son 1604.[19]

He died in 1612 and was buried at St Alphage's, Greenwich.

RICHARD WARNER Jnr

Appointed jointly with father 1604.[20]

On 30 August 1614, he was reappointed, along with his son Nowell, jointly as Master of the King's Barges.

In 1622 and 1624, Richard applied for certificates of residence in the Royal Household and not Blackheath. Presumably there was some financial advantage to being taxed within the Royal Household rather than his normal place of residence.[21]

NOWELL WARNER

Nowell Warner was originally appointed on 30 August 1614.

Nowell applied for Certificates of Residence within the Royal Household on numerous occasions, including 1626, 1629 and 1641.[22]

He was dismissed from his office by Parliament in 1648.

After the restoration of the monarchy, Nowell petitioned Charles II to be restored to his place. The petition was dated 12 May 1660.[23]

The King, upon reading the petition of Nowell Warner, Master of the Barge to King James and King Charles, 'which Place he enjoyed until 1648, and then was dismissed by Order of the House of Commons; therefore prayed he and his Fellowes might be restored to their Places again'. Which was accordingly ordered, until the King's pleasure to the contrary.[24]

On 18 March 1661, a money warrant for £30 was issued to Nowell Warner, as Master of His Majesty's Barges, as by letters patent of 30 August 1614, 'granting the said office to Richard Warner and Nowell Warner, said Nowell being still living and continued by the King in his office'.[25]

He was buried on 27 August 1662 at St Alphage's, Greenwich.

JOHN KELLOCK

John Kellock was Master of the Barge to Charles, Duke of York (later to become Charles I).

He is named in 1610 as the Master of the Barge in a list of the Duke of York's servants, whose wages are to be paid from 1 January that year. He was paid £18 6s 8d.[26]

He is still Master of the Prince's Barge in 1622 according to payments authorised by Robert Carey, Chamberlain of the Court of the Prince of Wales.[27]

He was appointed on 7 February 1626 for life, with a salary of £30 per annum.[28]

He had a certificate for taxation in the Royal Household in 1626.[29]

John Kellock died in 1627, leaving bequests to his family but also £5 a year to the poor of 'the ould Paris garden', the site of the Royal Bargehouse.

ROBERT CLEARKE

The Admiralty Muster/Census of the Thames watermen of 2 February 1628[30] gives Robert Clearke and Nowell Warner as Masters of the King's Barge. There are other men in the muster described as 'King's Servants'.

ROBERT BURSEY

He was a Ruler (presumably of the Watermen's Company). He was involved in the 1648 petition together with Nowell Warner.

Civil War

A large number of Royal Watermen and indeed the Royal Bargemaster himself were royalists and suffered for their loyalty to the Crown during the Interregnum.

When the Civil War broke out in 1642, Nowell Warner was Master of the Barges to Charles I. During that year he had arguments with the revolution-aries in the Watermen's Company. He was fiercely royalist and in 1648 he became involved with royalist agitation and conspiracy.

He was dismissed from his post by Parliament but reinstated by Charles II on his return to England.[31]

No.8 – To acquaint Sir M Livesey with the information given against Warner, the king's bargeman and one Mr Arthur. That he restrain the men and seize all arms belonging to them and certify the result to this Committee.[32]

From Adm. Com. To Robert Blackborne Navy Commander: Order to make out a bill to Rich. Nutt, master of the barges £10 10s for carrying Gen Bake to Gravesend and the Hope, and Gen Montague to Lamb, with the 10 oar barge. With Nutt's bill endorsed.

When Oliver Cromwell was buried on Thursday, 23 November 1658, he had a huge state funeral. It started from Somerset House in the Strand and processed to Westminster Abbey. In the procession was Richard Nutt, Master of the Barges, accompanied by twenty-eight watermen.[33]

26 January – Thomas Washbourne to be Assistant to the Barges.

27 January – Edward Leaman to be Master of the Barges.

RICHARD NUTT

Not actually a Royal Bargemaster as appointed during the Interregnum.

CSP Dom 1655/6 – described as Master of the Barges (order for payment to him dated 25 April 1656). On 28 April 1658 he received £8 0s 0d 'for fetching up the Dutch Ambassador', and on 8 September that year £44 16s for carrying the Duc de Crequy.

Nutt was paid £34 9s for attending the Swedish Ambassador from Dorset House to Whitehall and back and to Gravesend on 23–25 August 1658.

On 23 November 1658 he took part in the funeral procession of Oliver Cromwell, as Master of the Barges, accompanied by twenty-eight Watermen.

Richard Nutt's will was made on 20 June 1659 and proved on 13 August 1660. He came from Lambeth, and left a wife and children.[34]

THOMAS LEAMAN

Not actually a Royal Bargemaster, as appointed during the Interregnum. Appointed on 27 January 1659/60 by Warrant of the Council of State to be Master of the Barges.

THOMAS WASHBOURNE (Deputy to Richard Nutt)

Not actually a Royal Bargemaster as appointed during the Interregnum. Appointed on 26 January 1659/60 by Warrant of the Council of State to be Assistant to the Barges. He was witness to the will of Richard Nutt in 1660.

The Restoration of The Monarchy in 1660

After King Charles II was restored to the throne, a number of petitions were received by the Lord Chamberlain's department requesting posts in his household, including the following:

No. 67 Walter Grant. His Majesty's Waterman. For the place of Master of the Barge. Was the first who wore his livery, and is the eldest Waterman in the service.

No. 68 George KirPaterick, Waterman. For a place in his Majesty's barge. Served the late King 16 years by sea and land in the wars; was often imprisoned, twice tried for life and three times forbidden his employment and banished the river.

No. 69 Charles Stuart, of London, Waterman. For the place of Bargeman to his Majesty.

NOWELL WARNER (see also earlier entry)

Nowell Warner was originally appointed in 1614. On 18 March 1660/61 a money warrant for £30 was issued to Nowell Warner, as Master of His Majesty's Barges, as by letters patent of 30 August 1614, granting the said office to Richard Warner and Nowell Warner. It said Nowell was still living and was continued by the King in his office.

On 12 May 1660 he was restored to office.[35]

After the restoration of the monarchy, Nowell petitioned Charles II to be restored to his place. The petition was dated 15 May 1660.

He was buried on 27 August 1662 at St Alphage's, Greenwich.

JOHN WARNER

John Warner was the son of Nowell Warner.

He was appointed on 13 February 1661 to be Royal Bargemaster alongside his father. This is evidenced by a money warrant dated 15 May 1661 for £30 to John Warner, appointed by letters patent of 13 February 1660, in which he is described as Master of His Majesty's Barges together with Nowell Warner.[36]

He was appointed on 26 June 1663 in his own right. On the same day a money warrant was issued 'dormant for the fee of £30 per ann to John Warner as master of His Majesty's Barges, loco his father Nowell Warner deceased'.[37]

DANIEL HILL

Daniel Hill was appointed on 12 May 1685.

We have little detail of Hill's time as Royal Bargemaster as he was in office for such a short time. He died at Lambeth on 24 May 1687 and his will was proved the following month. He died a wealthy man, leaving, among other things, six tenements in Lambeth Marsh, a tenement in New Tuttle Street in Westminster, two tenements in Charlton in Kent, a barge and a bargehouse.[38]

JOHN WARNER Snr

Appointed Royal Waterman on 9 September 1678, he was appointed Royal Bargemaster to the Queen Consort *c.*1686 and as Royal Bargemaster on 29 May 1687.

It would appear he was also Master of the Barge to the Queen Consort prior to his appointment as Master of the Barges to the King. There is a Royal Sign Manual dated 27 October 1686 for £75 4s 9d to John Warner, Master of the Barges to the Queen Consort, for 6 per cent interest for one year to 29 September on £1,254 due to him on an order No. 781, registered on the Hearth Money for two houses at Greenwich, bought off him by Charles II.[39]

On 14 June 1687 there was another Royal Sign Manual to pay £60 per annum to John Warner, 'whom the King has appointed to be Master of the Barges loco Daniell Hill deceased; same to be payable quarterly as from Lady Day last during pleasure'.[40]

He died in April 1694 and was buried on 23 April 1694 at St Alphage's, Greenwich.

JOHN WARNER Jnr

Appointed on 17 April 1694, he was a Waterman on 18 June.

In 1711 he was paid £78 12s 6d for carrying the crown to Parliament House and for carrying goods to Hampton Court and Windsor.[41]

John Warner Jnr died between 30 April and 2 May 1713. He made his will on 30 April 1713 and it was proved on 2 May that year. He was buried on 10 May at St Alphage's, Greenwich.

CHRISTOPHER HILL

Christopher Hill was appointed as Master of the Barges to Queen Mary II on 1 May 1689. He was still in her service when she died on 28 December 1694.

In 1711 he is described as Bargemaster to the late Prince Consort.[42]

He was appointed on 7 May 1713 as Master of the Barges. Prior to his appointment, it seems he was Bargemaster to Queen Anne's husband, Prince George of Denmark, who died on 28 October 1708. After the prince's death he tried to claim his barge as a fee and perquisite of his place.[43]

On 31 March 1712, Sir John Stanley sent the following to Spencer Compton:

Sir, Her Majestie having been pleased to refer my Lord Chamberlain the inclosed peticon of Mr Hill, master of the barges to his late Royall Highness [Prince George of Denmark], his Grace desires you to inform him what allowance was made to Mr Hill out of your office for repairs to the barges, barge-house etc, and to what time paid. Also to inform him whether the Prince's barge do now belong to her Majestie, or [can be] claimed as a fee by any of his officer.

He was still in office in 1717, when he was paid £100 in lieu of allowances for the period 25 December 1716 to 25 December 1717.[44]

He died in 1718. His PCC (Prerogative Court of Canterbury) will was proved on 10 March 1718, and he left most of his estate to his brother John Hill of Lambeth, described as a Waterman.

JOHN HILL

Brother of Christopher Hill, he is mentioned as Master of the Barges when he is paid £150 for his services for eighteen months up to Christmas 1716. Perhaps at this point he was deputy, as Christopher Hill is also mentioned in the same payments list and also described as Master of the Barges.

He submitted his bill for the King's 'Water Music' party, carrying His Majesty from Whitehall to Chelsea on 17 July 1717. The bill was for £3 10*d* ('The Shallope' £1, the twelve-oared barge £1, the eight-oared barge £1 and the six-oared barge 10d).

He was appointed on 27 February 1719 as Royal Bargemaster, which office he held until 1727.

ROBERT MASON

Appointed on 14 September 1727, in September 1729 he was granted new liveries for himself and forty-eight Watermen, with a similar grant being made in September 1734.[45]

He died in March 1736 and was succeeded by his son John. His will, which was made in 1733, was proved on 3 April 1736. It left property in Stangate and Wall End to his wife Sarah. He left several hundred pounds each to his sons Robert, William, John, Jervas and Benjamin, and his daughters Sarah, Mercy and Elizabeth. Mercy and Elizabeth were underage when their father died, so he requested that William Church, Clerk of Watermans Hall, invest their legacies for them until they reached 18 years of age. There were also a number of personal bequests of silver to most of the children.

JOHN MASON

He was appointed on 30 March 1736.

On flat stones at Lambeth Church is an inscription to the memory of John Mason, Esq., who died in 1768, saying 'he was bargemaster to the late King and his present Majesty'.

John's will was proved on 12 April 1768. In it he directs his executors and trustees to have a vault built in the new churchyard belonging to the Parish of Lambeth. He then goes on, 'As it is usual for His Majesty's Watermen to attend the Barge Master's funeral I hereby give to such of them as think proper to attend my funeral a pair of gloves and that my executors give to each of them two shillings and six pence.' He makes bequests to his brothers and nieces and nephews. However, the main beneficiary would appear to be his nephew Robert Mason, the son of his late brother Robert, to whom he leaves freehold land and property in Greenwich and leasehold land and property in Lambeth.

During John Mason's tenure, Richard Scott was Master of the Barges to the Queen and therefore probably served as his deputy.

ROBERT MASON

Appointed on 2 May 1768, he was the nephew of John Mason, also a Royal Bargemaster.

Robert was a resident of Lambeth, as were a number of other Royal Bargemasters. He died in 1773, his will being proved on 23 April that year.

WILLIAM SAWYER

Appointed on 15 September 1767 as Waterman,[46] he became Royal Bargemaster on 23 March 1773.

He had a tragedy in his life shortly before his death:

Mrs Ann Sawyer, wife of Mr William Sawyer, the King's barge-master, at his house, Bishop's Walk, Lambeth. Some villains had first broke open the house, and packed up all the valuables they could find; but Mrs Sawyer hearing a noise in the house, had got up to see what was the matter, when they knocked her down, stabbed her in several places, and put one of her eyes out, which noise awoke the servant, and she got up and called the watch, when they all made off in a boat, without their booty.[47]

RICHARD ROBERTS

Appointed on 16 November 1796, he was also Keeper of the King's Swans in 1793.

Richard Roberts resigned on 6 January 1808 in favour of his nephew Thomas Alexander Roberts.[48] He submitted the following letter to the Lord Chamberlain:

The Right Hon the Earl of Dartmouth, Lord Chamberlain to His Majesty, having at the request of several of my great and good Friends, Assisting my most respectfull solicitation to His Lordship, that His Lordship would please to give me Leave to resign my situation of Barge Master to the King on Behalf of my Nephew Thomas Alexander Roberts, which request His Lordship having to permit me to Do, in favour of my said Nephew, I hereby most gratefully beg leave to humbly thank His Lordship, and to resign my Situation of Master of the King's Barges Accordingly with the greatest respect.

His Lordships Most Obedient humble Servant Richard Roberts

The King's Bargehouse,

Lambeth 6th January 1808

THOMAS ALEXANDER ROBERTS

Prior to his appointment as Royal Bargemaster on 14 July 1808, he submitted the following letter of resignation as Royal Waterman to the Lord Chamberlain:

Having this the recommendation of Our Great and Kind Friends, to His Lordship pleased to Accept of my Uncle's resignation in my Favour, Appointing me Bargemaster to His Majesty, for which I humbly Trust I shall always be most truly thankfull. Having had the honor Several years of being One of the King's Watermen. The great honor to which by his Loodships Goodness I am now Succeeding to, my Resignation as being one of His Majesty's Watermen is most thankfully and Dutifully mentioned by, May it please His Lordship

His Lordships Most Respectfully Obedient Servant

Thomas Alexander Roberts

The King's Bargehouse Lambeth

January 6th 1808

The warrant appointing his successor, John Roberts, says he resigned. He was also Keeper of Swans and Cygnets.

He died in 1837, leaving a PCC will. In the will, which had been made on 2 January 1836 and was proved on 3 March 1837, he describes himself as a boatbuilder. He asks to be buried in the family vault in Lambeth Churchyard and, like his uncle, wants 'no pomp or parade' at his funeral. He leaves leasehold bargehouses, boathouses and warehouses situated in Archbishop's Walk, together with barges, boats and stocks of timber, to his sons John and William Roberts so long as they continue to carry on business as boatbuilders. He leaves property in Fore Street, Lambeth, to his son Thomas Alexander Roberts. There are various other bequests to his wife and family.

JOHN ROBERTS

Appointed on 28 October 1846, his warrant states that he took over from Thomas Alexander Roberts, who had resigned. He was also appointed Keeper of The Swans and Cygnets on the same day. This was again as successor to T. A. Roberts.

JAMES ARTHUR MESSENGER

James Arthur Messenger served as Royal Bargemaster from 1856–1901.

He set up a boatbuilding business on a site near to the Anglers Hotel in Teddington. He later built a large boathouse on the same site, where the Royal Barge and Shallop were housed.

The original warrant of appointment says he was to commence in the role on 3 August 1860. He replaced John Roberts, who had died.

Messenger was born in 1826 at Teddington, and was appointed a Royal Waterman in 1856.

In September 1897, he was informed of Queen Victoria's intention of presenting the Jubilee medal to all of her Watermen.[49]

Messenger died aged 75 at his home in Teddington on 21 June 1901 whilst still in office as HM Bargemaster.

On the picture overleaf, note the 'V' and 'R' lettering on the plastron of his uniform. As the Bargemaster's appointment is personal to the monarch, on the death of the King or Queen the post becomes vacant and reappointment, or a new appointment, is required. The lettering on the plastron then changes to that of the new monarch.

Right: Letter from HM Bargemaster James
Messenger to Richard Turk (future Bargemaster)
on his appointment as HM Waterman. (Picture
from the Turk family collection)

Below: J.A. Messenger, with R. Turk on the right
and W. Biffin on the left. (Picture from the Turk
family collection)

WILLIAM GILES EAST

HM Bargemaster from 1901–33, William 'Bill' Giles East was baptised on 11 March 1866 at St Mary's, Lambeth, the son of William East, a boatbuilder.

By the time of the 1871 census, the family had moved to Putney. They were still there in 1881, their address given as East's Boat House, Leander Rowing Club, Putney. In 1882 he was apprenticed to a waterman.

He won the Doggett's Coat and Badge Race in 1887 and the English Sculling Championship in 1891.

At the time of the 1891 census, he was living with his parents at the Coach and Horses, Richmond Road, Isleworth.

He gave his profession as a professional sculler, his father now described as a licensed victualler.

William was appointed a Royal Waterman in 1898. The census of 31 March/1 April 1901 shows him living at the Prince's Head in Richmond, his profession given as licenced victualler.

In June 1901, he was appointed as the Royal Bargemaster.

He gave an interview to A. Wallis Myers that was published in *The Black and White Illustrated Budget* on 28 September 1901. Asked what his job entailed, he said, 'Roughly speaking I have to take charge of the Watermen, pay them their fees, and superintend their work.' He told the interviewer that he was paid £60 per annum plus a daily fee when on duty, but that the Watermen only got £5 per annum plus their daily fee. He mentioned having to carry the crown to the Chamber Door for the State Opening of Parliament. He also recounted that last spring, when he was still only a Waterman, he and three other Watermen were deputed to carry a mace.

By 1911 he had moved to the Pigeons Hotel in Richmond as its proprietor. By this period in its history, the role of Royal Bargemaster was no longer a full-time occupation.

He was in charge of the Royal Barge when King George V and Queen Mary attended Henley Royal Regatta in 1912. An article appeared in *The Dominion* on 20 August 1912, which described the occasion beautifully:

The stately old craft came slow and serenely through the dark arches of the bridge. The gold badges on the backs of the scarlet oarsmen shone bravely as they swung, and there, bending their heads to look out from under the gold canopy of the awning were the King and Queen and Princess Mary,

William East, a future Royal Bargemaster, shown here with HM Bargemaster Ernest Barry and Richard Turk, also a future Bargemaster. (Picture from the Turk family collection)

HM Bargemaster Bill East at Henley, with the King and Queen aboard the Royal Barge. (Public domain image)

smiling with delight at the fairest scene the Thames had known for many a year.

Down to the white pavilion on the Berkshire bank they swept, the King's Bargemaster, Mr William East, craning his neck to peer over the awning roof and steering cunningly with the tiller between his knees … after tea the Queen gave away the prizes, and then the procession by water back to the station brought a perfect day to its ending.

He and his Royal Watermen used to row guests at the Royal garden parties around the lake at Buckingham Palace. His last great ceremonial occasion was in 1919, when he was in charge of the barge that took the King from the Tower of London to Chelsea during a pageant.

William East died at the Pigeons Hotel in Petersham Road, Richmond, Surrey, on 10 December 1932.

On 12 October 2015, the oars he used when winning the English Sculling Championship came up for auction but fetched a mere £70.

JOHN THOMAS PHELPS (known best as 'Bossie' Phelps)

John Thomas 'Bossie' Phelps was appointed Royal Bargemaster in February 1933 by George VI.

Born at Putney in 1877, he was the son of John Thomas 'Old Bossie' Phelps, a well-known boat builder, who had himself been appointed as a Royal Waterman in 1888. The Phelps family were a famous dynasty of boatbuilders and rowers.

In 1894, 'Bossie' was apprenticed to his father as a boatbuilder. He continued to try to develop the business, Bowers, Phelps & Sons, taking over from his father, who died in 1910.

Young 'Bossie' had come third in the Doggett's race in 1899. His father, not best pleased with his son's efforts, is alleged to have taken young 'Bossie' to the foreshore in Putney after the race and said, 'You see that river son? Well you will be the last of my family to lose on it.' What effect his father's homily had upon young 'Bossie' can only be guessed at, but he became a larger-than-life character, both forceful and charismatic.

'Bossie' married Emily Maud Lamble Ferris in 1903, and their union produced two surviving sons, Ted and Eric.

The First World War was very profitable for the family boatbuilding business, 'Bossie' becoming a major contractor to the War Office and the Admiralty. They also continued to build boats for the rowing community.

In the interwar years, 'Bossie' continued to run the boatbuilding business but at the same time became the most sought-after rowing coach in the country. Under his management, his son Ted won Doggett's in 1930, while his other son Eric won it in 1933. He trained nine winners of the Diamond Sculls and nine of the Amateur Championship (the Wingfield Sculls).

At the age of 18, Ted won the Newcastle Handicap, which at the time was the prime professional race in northern England. Two years later, in 1928, Ted went to South America for a coaching job in Montevideo, but returned to London in 1930 to challenge Ernest Barry's nephew, Bert Barry, for the World Professional Sculling Championship title. Ted won the title –

Above left: 'Bossie' Phelps in HM Bargemaster's uniform. Note the uniform plastron at that time was coloured in some parts. (Picture from the Turk family collection)

Above right: 'Bossie' Phelps presenting prizes at Putney Regatta. (Picture from the Phelps family collection)

doing so three times in all – and three months later he entered the Thomas Doggett's Coat and Badge Race, which is the oldest rowing race in the world, instigated by the Irish comedy actor Thomas Doggett and sculled for the first time in 1715 on the Thames. Ted Phelps did not have a difficult time winning this race. Winning Doggett's was normally a good start to your professional rowing career, where the pinnacle might have been to crown it with the world title. Ted Phelps did it in the reverse order, which was very unusual. Eric Phelps was also the English Sculling Champion twice.

With his appointment as Royal Bargemaster, 'Bossie' reached the pinnacle of his career, although coaching and boatbuilding took up most of his time as there were only the ceremonial duties of a Royal Bargemaster to attend to. According to Hylton Cleaver, the following happened when 'Bossie' was leading his Royal Watermen in a procession:

> [A] Marshal came up on his prancing steed, mustering parties into place for the march and signalling Bossie to bring his men into line. Bossie was neither a landsman nor a soldier. He was beaten for words of command. So he addressed his crew in the only way they would understand: Ready? Forward all! Paddle!

The Second World War was not so kind to his boatbuilding business, as they did not get the war work they had enjoyed during the First World War. The business collapsed, leaving 'Bossie' with large debts. He and his wife went to live in Torcross, Devon, where he died aged 64 in 1942 while still serving as Royal Bargemaster. Members of his family would joke, 'If anyone asks whether you are related to Bossie – always say "No". He died owing so much money, they would have the shirt off your back.'

If you contemplate rowing. Remember,
When you know all about it, you will be too old to do it.

RICHARD H. TURK

The office of HM Bargemaster was not filled until 1946 – presumably because of the war – when Richard H. Turk was appointed on 17 October.

The letter of his appointment says he was appointed as HM Bargemaster in succession to 'Bossie' Phelps, but for only two years. Presumably the

Richard Turk, HM Bargemaster. (Picture from the Turk family collection)

Richard Turk in uniform of Vintners' Bargemaster and Company Swan Marker. Swan Uppers traditionally display a swan's white feather in their cap. The term 'upper' probably comes from the name given to river trades who worked up-river of London Bridge. He was also the Vintner Company Bargemaster. He held this position from 1904–60. A remarkable period of time to hold the role. He must have witnessed many significant changes to the Thames during this period. (Permission from the Vintner's Company)

two-year appointment was because of his age, although in fact he stayed in the post until 1948/49.

There is a Getty image online showing him being fitted for a new uniform for the State Opening of Parliament.

There is also a newspaper article regarding the 1946 State Opening of Parliament which says it marked the return of pageantry to London after the war.

Richard H. Turk had his last engagement at the State Opening of Parliament in 1948.

ERNEST BARRY

Ernest Barry, shown overleaf in 1950, was appointed HM Bargemaster in January 1949 and retired in 1952. An extremely good rower and sculler, he was born in 1882.

Ernest Barry shown wearing a boater and being escorted by mounted police on the towpath at Putney, 21 July 1913.

Ernest Barry shown in sculling boat. (Picture from the Turk family collection)

He won the Doggett's Coat and Badge Race in 1903. He also competed in the World Professional Sculling Championship, which took place on the Zambezi River in Africa, which unfortunately he did not win. However, he did win the championship when it was held on the River Thames in 1912.

On 21 July 1913, Ernest Barry made an attempt to retain the world title over the Thames Championship course between Putney and Mortlake against Harry Pearce of Australia for a prize of £500. Barry won the race in a time of 24 minutes and 9 seconds.

Twenty years later in 1933, Harry Pearce's son, Bobby, would take the world title from Ted Phelps. Bobby Pearce had begun his sculling career as an amateur, taking two Olympic gold medals in the singles in 1928 and 1932, and the Diamonds at Henley in 1931.

Barry actually won the title every year for five years, before losing it but finally regaining it in Australia in 1920.

Ernest Barry was made a Royal Waterman in 1913. It was the working waterman's job to row people across the Thames in the days when there were fewer bridges. He went away to fight in the First World War before returning to live in Twickenham with his wife Lotte, one of the Hammerton family that lived at 25 The Embankment, the current location of the Twickenham Museum.

Ernest and Lotte Barry had five children and lived in Bonser Road, Twickenham. Ernest died in 1968 at the age of 86.

IV

BARGEMASTERS TO HM QUEEN ELIZABETH II

Her Majesty The Queen is unique among all English monarchs in the number of Bargemasters she has appointed during her long reign. To date there are six men who have held this appointment, and they are listed here with a more detailed individual background for each to illustrate their particular involvement with the River Thames fraternity.

HM the Queen at Watermen's Hall to celebrate the 800th anniversary of her Royal Watermen since Magna Carta in 1215. (R.G. Crouch collection, picture by Alex Savile)

During the joint celebrations for the Watermen's Company's quincentenary and the Royal Watermen's 800th anniversary since Magna Carta, the Queen honoured the Company and her Watermen with a visit to Watermen's Hall in the City of London.

The special photograph on the previous page was taken with the Queen and the Duke of Edinburgh, Her Majesty's serving watermen in uniform, retired Extra Watermen and past Royal Bargemasters. They are seated in the Freemen's room of the Watermen's historic Georgian Hall.

HERBERT ARTHUR (BERT) BARRY MVO

HM Bargemaster 1952–77

Her Majesty's first Bargemaster, Bert Barry, was appointed by the Queen in August 1952, aged 49, then the youngest Royal Bargemaster ever appointed. He was the nephew of Ernest Barry, who had recently retired from the post aged 70.

Bert retired at the end of the Queen's Silver Jubilee in 1977.

Bert Barry marshalling Royal Watermen's guard of honour. He was the first Bargemaster appointed by HM the Queen. (Picture from the Turk family collection)

Bert Barry (1902–78) was the son of W.A. 'Bill' Barry, who won Doggett's Coat and Badge Race in 1891 and was the Professional Sculling Champion of England in 1898.

Bert was a nephew of the great Ernest Barry and uncle of William L. 'Bill' Barry, winner of a silver medal in the coxless fours at the 1964 Olympics. Bert won Doggett's Coat and Badge in 1925, and in 1927 he challenged the World Professional Sculling Champion, M.L. Goodsell, for his title. Strangely, the race took place in Vancouver, Canada, and not in Goodsell's native Australia. The defending champion beat Barry convincingly. However, in a return match over the same course three months later, it was the Englishman who was victorious, and he remained the unchallenged world champion for nearly three years.

Pathé News has an especially good sound film of Bert sculling with his brother Lou around this period.

Ted Phelps raced against Bert Barry for the British Championship between Putney and Mortlake on the Thames. Ted won, but then lost the title the next year to Bert's brother, Lou Barry.

Bert Barry was a lifelong teetotaller and a very generous sculling coach. His father, William Barry, owned a lighterage company that he sold to W.M. Cory, later to become Cory Environmental PLC.

EDWIN 'TED' HUNT MVO

HM Bargemaster 1978–90

Edwin 'Ted' Hunt was born on 23 March 1920 and was bound apprentice to his father as a waterman and lighterman of the River Thames in 1935, learning to tow Thames cargo barges with a rowing boat.

At that time, Ted recalled, there were 7,000 barges on the river and hundreds of tugs.

Following the outbreak of the Second World War, Ted volunteered as a sapper waterman in the Royal Engineers, and served at Narvik and in the Norwegian campaign in April–May 1940.

By 1944 he was commissioned as a captain and commanded fifteen of the Rhino ferries on Gold Beach on D-Day. In four months, sixty-four of these landing craft put ashore 93,000 units (tanks, guns and vehicles) and 440,000 tons of military stores. During the last six months of the war in Europe, together with the Dutch hydraulics engineer Lieutenant C.L.M.

Lambrechtsen van Ritthem, he advised the Chief Engineer Second Army, Brigadier 'Ginger' Campbell, on the 'opposed crossing of water obstacles', so that the longest floating Bailey bridge of the Second World War could be constructed at Gennep in the Netherlands. This bridge over the River Maas (Meuse) was 4,008ft (1,221m) long and was opened on 19 February 1945.

Ted Hunt, HM Bargemaster, at the Royal Mews, Buckingham Palace. (Picture by Reflections Photography)

Demobilised as a major, he returned to civilian life as a college lecturer in navigation and watermanship at the City & East London College in London from 1948 until 1985. As a Royal Waterman, he was appointed Queen's Bargemaster in 1978, responsible for organising her Royal Watermen's duties. He retired from service as a Member of the Royal Victoria Order in 1990.

The Jackknifing of Carriage No. 5, on 16 April 1985, by E. Hunt

Some 30 years ago now, one of the state visits was that of the president of Malawi. One of the horses was very turbulent and caused a minor disaster. A few days later I got a letter from Peter Hartley who was Sir John's personal secretary. He remarked that he had not seen me at Windsor Castle the previous week and wondered what had happened. 'A light-hearted report from you would be very welcome.'

On receipt of my report he rang me and said that it had gone all round the Lord Chamberlain's office. I learned later that they had sent a copy to the Royal Mews and they in turn sent it to The Queen. I'm led to believe that Her Majesty was amused, as a result I stayed out of the Tower.

My Report
Windsor Castle: Lat. 51.27'N Long.0.36'W
Wind: Light and variable. High Water London Br 11.42 GMT.

Delay in the arrival of the President of Malawi on his State Visit caused Freddie, the horse lying second rank starboard, to attempt sitting down. At one stage he crossed legs and had a pronounced list to port, the postilion's starboard leg went in as a fender and no harm was done. Finally getting away from Home Park calmed him and we had no further trouble until we had the Guildhall on our port quarter and only half a cable of High Street remained.

Suddenly and for no apparent reason the horse ahead of Freddie reared up and attempted to shake hands with the postilion on his port side. There followed an uncontrollable rounding to port, without the requisite sound-signals and citizens of the Royal Borough and others scattered as the lead horses left the fairway and turned inshore over the pavement. One horse put a foot through a pushchair which fortunately was unladen. Remarkably the postilions were able to bring the team to a halt and a capsize was averted. Never without a compass, I noted that the carriage had a heading of 135, while the horses were 320. I knew instinctively that this was not right.

We have an arrangement that disasters of this sort require the starboard Waterman to see to the passengers, while the port Waterman sees to the horses. Nick Silvester, lying second-bottom to the brake, applied it to prevent our going ahead or astern, then leaped to the aid of our passengers, who had escaped injury.

The horses appeared to me to have grown in stature, but they were held so that the carriage could be careened over to allow traces to be pulled clear before Crown Equerry arrived to take command. With him was one Arthur, Head Coachman, bravely hiding his despair at having to rely on two ex-boat boys to release horses from carriage: there was not a bow-line or clove-hitch to be seen, so he declined our offers of assistance and wisely got on with the job himself. I am now reading a book on 'Harness'. A quick survey showed that the carriage had a broken main-shaft and a broken quadrant and would be lucky to be classified C3 at Lloyds. There were no apparent injuries to those ashore: our passengers headed for the Castle in a Rolls-Royce, and my inadequacies found me reluctant to look Crown Equerry in the eye.

When the horses were de-rigged the postilions dismounted and led their charges to a berth ashore at The Mews. A police officer then asked Arthur what he should do with the carriage. A pregnant pause, then Arthur suggested that the carriage had become a main-channel obstruction and it would be appreciated if lots of policemen towed it out of the fairway and back to its home port. Arthur then suggested that we three should go to lunch. On leaving the scene I could not deny myself the pleasure of looking back at those now dealing with the problem.

At St. George's Gate, Nick and I met Superintendent Royal Mews and the Comptroller, both anxious to learn the reason for their tally being one short. Asked if Freddie was to blame I was happy to pronounce Freddie innocent and added that the culprit had indeed been 'the horse in the starboard towrope'. I noticed that the maroon plumes carried by this Blues and Royals officer visibly shook at my reply, and I noticed that the Comptroller was kind enough to turn away before looking heavenwards in a silent plea for strength. At lunch I learned that the starboard towrope horse was one 'Rideau', and I resolved never to share a duty with him again.

Edwin Hunt. Bargemaster to Her Majesty.

'Under oars with Soverein aboard'

My predecessor as Queen's Bargemaster was Bert Barry, one-time world professional sculling champion, and when he retired at the end of Silver Jubilee Year I took over as skipper of 22 Royal Watermen. Throughout each year some of us were required to attend occasions involving members of the Royal Family. Today, many Royal Watermen's duties that used to take place afloat, such as royal weddings and state visits, have gone ashore, and these find us manning carriages instead of boats.

An event I especially remember was the state visit of Queen Beatrix of the Netherlands. She arrived at Greenwich in a Dutch warship and was taken by royal barge to Westminster Pier to be greeted by our Queen and a host of other royals, then by carriage – many in the procession manned by Royal Watermen – to Buckingham Palace.

In Port of London waters the launch *Royal Nore* normally plays the role of Royal Barge while in Thames Water areas it is the *Windrush*. The current Bargemaster is Paul Ludwig who had the pleasure of commanding *Gloriana* "under oars with Sovereign aboard" 95 years after the previous occasion. I was green with envy.

For 500 years the Bargemaster has been nominally responsible for getting the Imperial State Crown to Westminster for the state opening of parliament. In the 16th century the crown would be taken from Traitors' Gate to Hampton Court. Then, with the sovereign aboard, it would be rowed downriver to parliament, where the Bargemaster would carry it in.

Today we man carriages in two processions. The crown leaves Buckingham Palace on an illuminated table in a state coach with a regalia escort of Household Cavalry. At Westminster the Bargemaster hands it on while the Escorting Waterman handles the Great Sword of State.

During the Bargemaster's tour of office the Queen finds an opportunity to chat with the Bargemaster's wife. After twelve years I reached retirement age and received Her Majesty's gift of the Royal Victorian Order in the presence of my wife and two daughters.

Ted Hunt

Ted Hunt proudly wears the Légion d'honneur (furthest right in his row of medals) after receiving it at Watermen's Hall (Picture: Lancing Herald)

Left: A Rhino ferry of assembled pontoons 'married' to an LST (landing ship, tank) in 1944

Far left: Ted Hunt carrying the Imperial State Crown in to parliament, one of the Queen's Bargemaster's main responsibilities

The Great River Race 2016   Medal-mounting by Duchemins   33

(Personal collection of Ted Hunt)

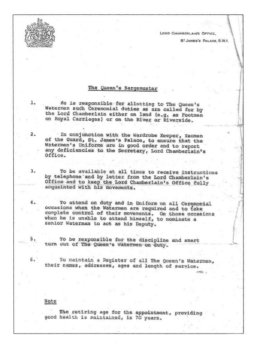

LORD CHAMBERLAIN'S OFFICE,
ST JAMES'S PALACE, S.W.I.

The Queen's Bargemaster

1. He is responsible for allotting to The Queen's Watermen such Ceremonial duties as are called for by the Lord Chamberlain either on land (e.g. as Footmen on Royal Carriages) or on the River or Riverside.

2. In conjunction with the Wardrobe Keeper, Yeomen of the Guard, St. James's Palace, to ensure that the Watermen's Uniforms are in good order and to report any deficiencies to the Secretary, Lord Chamberlain's Office.

3. To be available at all times to receive instructions by telephone and by letter from the Lord Chamberlain's Office and to keep the Lord Chamberlain's Office fully acquainted with his movements.

4. To attend on duty and in Uniform on all Ceremonial occasions when the Watermen are required and to take complete control of their movements. On those occasions when he is unable to attend himself, to nominate a senior Waterman to act as his Deputy.

5. To be responsible for the discipline and smart turn out of The Queen's Watermen on duty.

6. To maintain a Register of all The Queen's Watermen, their names, addresses, ages and length of service.

Note

The retiring age for the appointment, providing good health is maintained, is 70 years.

Letter of instructions received by Ted Hunt from the Palace in 1977 listing the duties of a Royal Bargemaster. (Personal collection of Ted Hunt)

Another event which I would like to relate from during my time as Bargemaster concerned the Duke of Edinburgh. A river visit by the Queen was arranged for Her Majesty to open the new Henley Regatta headquarters in the upper non-tidal Thames. The Royal Barge for this area is MV *Windrush*, as always manned for Her Majesty by her Bargemaster and eight Royal Watermen. The boat stopped at the Regatta landing stage, where the Royal Watermen disembarked and formed up as a Guard of Honour for the Queen to pass through to meet the local dignitaries. The usual routine was performed perfectly and I duly handed Her Majesty ashore followed by the Duke of Edinburgh. The local Mayor and his entourage, in their eagerness to meet the Queen, came forward very quickly and caused the Royal party to stop-short while still abreast of the Guard of Honour on the landing stage. The Duke, having been stopped in front of the honour guard looked questioningly at the Red-uniformed Watermen about him and enquiringly said, 'Can you chaps row?' The nearest man happened to be Ken Dwan, a double Olympic oarsman, on each side of whom were an assortment of international rowers and Henley participants. Ken Dwan, looking a bit shocked, replied 'Yes Sir, we can.' The Duke then, with a quizzical look on his face, moved on.

After the day's duty was over, the Royal Watermen assembled at their usual pub in Crown Ally near to St James's Palace, that we use for what we call our 'de-briefing', the topic of conversation was of course the Duke's comment. As the pints flowed and feelings kindled into a realisation that many people might wonder if we were merely decoration for the Royal Barge, it was decided that we should do something to show that we could match the pulling feats of the ancient Royal Watermen by rowing a meaningful distance. It was decided that we would undertake a marathon row from Hampton Court to Greenwich, a distance of about 30 miles. Mike Turk still had the replica Royal Shallop which had been built for the film [A] *Man for All Seasons* and so the idea was born.

At this time one of the Royal Watermen, Bob Crouch, was the Senior Warden at the Watermen's Co. Guild and as such was heavily involved with the arrangements for the event. We felt we needed something extra to add to the occasion, and he was able to persuade the Water Conservators Livery Company who shared Watermen's Hall at that time, to donate a slice of ancient timber water pipe as was used to provide water from the Thames to the citizens of London, [and] to this slice of water pipe Bob added a model of a seventeenth century working watermen seated in his wherry with a passenger carrying a miniature Stela in his lap. The diorama was enclosed in a glass transportation/presentation case.

We decided that we would deliver the Stela representing the many uses of London's river water, under oars from Palace to Palace to draw attention to the underused potential of the River Thames, we decided we would call it 'The Tudor Pull'.

The Tudor Pull Stela. (Picture by Reflections Photography)

The first Tudor Pull in 1986, rowed in the Royal Shallop built for the film *A Man For All Seasons*. (Picture by Sue Milton, photographer)

The event took place later that year and was such a success that it received a full front page picture and coverage in *The Times* newspaper. The idea caught on like wildfire and we were soon talking about the advantages of reintroducing this original type of fixed-seat rowing code as a sport for all ages and abilities, which we would call 'Traditional Rowing'. An association was set up and today this form of rowing for all comers has a great following. The intention had been to use The Tudor Pull as a one-off event, but due to the publicity it had attracted, the Watermen's Co. took the idea over and kept it going as an annual event involving City Livery Companies using their Cutters. They also started another annual fixed-seat event which they called the Great River Race, both of which are still rowed each year, the GRR now with some 300 competitors taking part. To this day, I don't think the Duke of Edinburgh knows what he started with that remark of his to the Royal Watermen.

ROBERT GEORGE (BOB) CROUCH MVO

HM Bargemaster 1990–2002

The model of *Royal Nore* was commissioned by Her Majesty's Watermen from Bob Crouch as their Golden Jubilee gift to Her Majesty. The Royal Barge *Nore* has been used by the Queen on the tidal reaches of the Thames throughout her reign.

Life and River Reminiscences by Bob Crouch

When looking back, I am amazed at the changes to the river environment within my lifetime, from the times when my father and grandfather used rowing boats to moor and attend on ships at Greenwich Buoys, to the water-jet Riverbus and the containerisation of ships' cargoes of today.

Being born into a Thames Watermen's family meant that from the very beginning various characteristics of the river would determine my future. I was once told that water is the 'universal carrier', able to convey the very smallest substances to the very largest floating objects. I have learnt that the Thames can also support the aspirations of its working men.

My first and most lasting memory of the river dates back to 1940 when London's docks and the river were under mortal attack from Hitler's war-

planes. At that time my parents and I were living on the Isle of Dogs, near to my mother's large family of Stevedores. On one memorable evening while we were hiding in the local communal shelter, our house was destroyed by a direct hit from a German bomb. I don't remember being frightened, but now if I think back at the terror and

Bob Crouch presenting the Royal Watermen's gift to Her Majesty on the occasion of her Golden Jubilee. (Picture by J. Borg Photography)

hopeless anxiety which must have been in the minds of my parents, it fills me with wonder at their outward calmness and self-control.

My father, who was on leave from his volunteer service in the Royal Navy at the time, decided to row my mother, me and our dog, across the river in his watermen's skiff, to his mother's house in Greenwich. I remember the river shining red, white and orange from the reflection of the fires and flames vigorously consuming the docks, wharves and vessels all about us, it seemed as if the water itself was alight. That image burnt itself into my 3-year-old memory and is still there to this day.

Now came the misty-memory of evacuation to a farm in Oxford, of moving to a new house in East Greenwich, of suffering another near miss from a Doodle-bug while Mother and I were in our Anderson shelter in the garden. Wonder and amazement brought me through to the end of the war, to a time of belated schooling at Halestow Road infants and the wild play we enjoyed in the bombed buildings situated everywhere about us. It was a time of strict rationing of food and other items, a hardship not acknowledged by us children, having not known anything else. After this war experience, it may seem bizarre that in later life I fell in love with and married a German lady who I met on an Austrian ski holiday.

The highlight of my early years after the war was going with my father to his work, attending ships moored at Greenwich Buoys. I was allowed to sit in the bow of his watermen's skiff and watch as he rowed the gangs of Stevedores out to the ships to unload the massive three hundredweight bags of sugar, or the heavy mysterious boxes of cargo into Lighters clustered around the moored ship, looking like hungry piglets at their mother's teats. These men seemed to me like friendly giants, dressed in leather jerkins with their hefty wooden-handled iron hooks tucked into thick brass-buckled belts. They would tease and joke with me, asking when I would be big enough to row the boat, and they would sometimes give me a coin or two.

At eleven I moved on to my senior school 'Charlton Central School for Boys' which proved to be quite a shock to the system. Discipline and corporal punishment were rife. In fact during the almost six years that I was there, I was caned on twenty-one occasions, and to think I was one of the better behaved and more obedient pupils.

It was also at this time that I learnt about the 'work ethic'. In my last year at school I did a paper-round every morning before school started, another shorter round in the evening, followed by selling the *News, Star* or *Standard* at the Charlton Tram Depot to the frantic, impatient workers as they streamed out to catch their trams or trains for home.

On Saturday mornings I worked as a Horse-boy for the Royal Arsenal Bakery Co. in Powis Street, Woolwich and went out with the horse-drawn delivery vans to help with the more livery animals. I can still remember the wonderful smell of the newly-baked bread, particularly on cold winter mornings, only sometimes offset by the exhausts emanating from the stern-end of the horse.

Sundays, after delivering the Sunday papers over my Blackheath paper-round, I had to return over the same round to collect the money owed to Mr Walsh the newspaper shop owner. I was in fact earning more money during my last year at school than in my first year at work.

After being forced by my father to stay on at school for an extra year to take my School Certificate Exams, I entered the world of work. There was some disagreement with father, who, because I had passed my SCEs, wanted me to become a Draftsman for a Bridge Building company owned by a friend of his, but in the end I won the day and he agreed to bind me for the five year apprenticeship to the trade of a Thames Watermen and Lightermen.

At this time my sporting interests were in swimming and playing water-polo for Greenwich Swimming Club. However, during this time of work for Silvertown Services Ltd the water transport wing of Tate and Lyle, I became interested in rowing and at father's insistence I entered for the coveted Doggett's Coat and Badge Wager, a specialised professional sculling race for young watermen first rowed for in 1715. This led me to my first encounter with a Royal Waterman.

My father had arranged for me to be trained for the race by Mr Jack West who was to be my coach for the only chance I had of entering the race at the end of my apprenticeship in 1958. After two years or so with Jack's hard training regime, for my final intense coaching he sent me to Barnes, to a famous world champion sculler and Royal Waterman called Bert Barry (later to become Her Majesty's Bargemaster). I had been out of action due to a hernia operation six months before the race, therefore these last three intensive months were extremely important for my only chance of winning. The day of the race was in late July of 1958, and after some unnerving moments during the race, I was fortunate enough to win Mr Doggett's wager.

Royal Barge at Old Swan Inn, Chelsea, the finish of the Doggett's Coat and Badge Wager race.

Having been deferred from National Service to allow me to finish my apprenticeship, I now had to suffer impressment into the Royal Navy for two years. In the event I have to admit that I enjoyed the experience, even considering a suggestion by the Captain of my ship HMS *Battleaxe*, to sign-on full time and enter an officer's training course. However, the call of the river won me back and I returned to my first love the Thames, and going into partnership with my father as an Attendance Waterman for Greenwich Buoys. Being a restless soul, I soon branched out into Bridge Piloting. I also took up my rowing career again and competed at the Henley Royal Regattas in 1960, '61 and '62.

In 1962, with my wife Ursula and our new daughter Nathalie to support, I bought into a newly formed pleasure-boat company called Catamaran Cruisers Ltd. While building the business over the next twenty-seven years, I also became Managing Director of 'Thames Line' a new Riverbus Co. During this period my involvement with the Watermen's Co. led me to become Master in 1987.

With the help and assistance of Major Ted Hunt I offered my services to HM The Queen as a Royal Waterman and was delighted when in 1981

I was appointed. My first Royal Duty was as a carriage-box rider on the coach carrying the Regalia Maces for the State Opening of Parliament. I was partnered with Ken Dwan, an experienced RW. We climbed up onto the stern of the carriage and Ken whispered to me. 'As we drive out through the Palace gates it will be an experience that you will never forget.' He was right, even though I have been involved with many wonderful duties and events over the years. That first time leaving Buckingham Palace and passing through the cheering crowds outside is beyond deception.

It was in 1990 that Ted Hunt, who had become Her Majesty's Bargemaster, retired at age 70 years. As was his right, he had chosen four men from the ranks of serving Royal Watermen to put forward as his replacement and I was one of them. We were all interviewed at the Palace by the Comptroller Col West with his intended replacements Col Ross and with Ted Hunt sitting in at the meetings. You can imagine my delight when I received a letter from The Queen's Secretary stating that Her Majesty had instructed him to offer me the appointment of HM Bargemaster.

The first thing I had to do was to organise a retirement party for Ted Hunt, and with the Royal Watermen's approval I used my hobby, later to become a profitable side-line business, to produce a model Royal Shallop to be presented to Ted as our gift at his retirement party, which was to be held on a Thames pleasure boat.

Now fully in office, I had to come to terms with my various duties which included organising the Royal Watermen for the State Opening of Parliament, State visits, and various river duties. I received a lot of advice from Ted Hunt, but decided to organise some things in my own way. Each Royal Waterman only did two or three duties each year and I wanted to give each man a fair chance of doing the full range of events. I also wanted to persuade the Privy Purse Office to allow some changes. I wanted permission to design a Royal Watermen's tie. I wanted to get agreement for us to wear the Royal Coat of Arms as a blazer badge and I wanted to change the lace-up shoes the Watermen wore for a gold buckle style. Col Ross was now in charge at the Palace and I found him to be a very agreeable person to work with. He readily agreed to all the changes I suggested.

On one occasion when we were interviewing men for potential new appointments, Col Ross asked me about some of the men's work as Lightermen, in particular the men working for Cory Lighterage who had mentioned a place called 'Mucking'. I explained that Mucking Sands was

Cory Environmental Thames tug en route to Rainham, Essex.

a place in the Thames Estuary where Cory Ltd delivered waste material from London for Landfill and Reclamation. He was obviously fascinated with the Lightermen's work and I said that if he could afford a whole day away from his Palace duties, I could arrange a trip on a Cory Tug to see how these men used their Lighterage skills in handling the large 500 ton barges, plus a towing visit to Mucking by tug. He agreed to this and on the prearranged day we met at Wandsworth Wharf at 7 a.m. to join the tug and to watch how the men collected the barges together using only the power of the tide and make them up into a tow formation ready for the tug and their voyage down river to the Thames Estuary.

The trip was a great success. Col Ross got on with everybody, his army officer training meant that he was obviously very used to dealing with men and put everyone at their ease. He told them something of his job as Comptroller at the Palace and about his Royal duties.

Even with the tide, the trip took five hours to reach Mucking Sands, but fortified with pint-mugs of tea and lots of Tug-Grub we eventually arrived and watched the barges being placed onto mooring buoys in readiness to be unloaded.

I had decided to give the Colonel a surprise thrill for the return trip, and had arranged with RW Ken Dwan to take us back to London on one of his fast water-Jet taxi-boats, a trip of about 90 minutes at 25 knots.

It was a most successful and useful day. Col Ross said it had showed him how skilful the work of his watermen/Lightermen was, and it had also allowed working men a glimpse into his Royal Household world.

On another occasion as Royal Bargemaster, I was asked to attend with Royal Waterman Mike Turk at Hampton Court to discuss the possibility of transporting a VIP bride to her wedding at Hampton Court by river, using the oared Shallop which Mike's company had originally built for the film *A Man for All Seasons*. On arrival at Hampton Court, we found that we were meeting the King of Spain and his entourage and that it was the wedding of his daughter that was being planned. During the meeting, the King unexpectedly asked if he could see the vessel and so we all left in a fleet of cars to visit Mike's yard at Sunbury.

Mike was not known for the tidiness of his place of work and the Yard Manager was not expecting a visit from a King. The place was full of working activity, the yard being littered with wood-shavings, open pots of paint with dried out paintbrushes resting on their tops. There were planks of wood and an array of rusty tools lying about. Mike ran ahead and was able to at least get his men to stop the noise they were making and to moderate their language. I had to gingerly hand the King over various obstacles and we finally reached the corner of the yard where the boat was kept under a tattered and torn cover. Mike then threw back the cover to reveal the sad-looking and neglected Shallop, creating a great cloud of dust in the process which caused us all to cough and splutter.

On returning to Hampton Court there was a noticeable change in the atmosphere of the meeting, the happy and wonderful idea of creating a magnificent arrival of the bride by Royal Shallop on her great day had subsided. Mike did his best to assure all concerned that the boat would be ready and turned out in all her glory on the day, but I could see on the faces in the room that there was concern. I was told a few days later that the idea had been dropped due to concerns over security.

In the year 2000 the great Millennium celebrations were to take place, the highlight of this was to be a river progress by the Queen from the Pool of London to Greenwich and I was afforded the magnificent honour of transporting Her Majesty down to the Millennium Dome at Greenwich to view a spectacular performance in the newly built tent-like structure. We were to use one of the City Cruisers Ltd pleasure boats as the Royal Barge, she being large enough to carry the 100 specially invited passengers.

Before the trip, the Queen would light a beacon from aboard this vessel while moored outside of the Tower of London which would set off a chain of fire-beacons to run across the country.

On the day, there were some nail-biting moments on-board as some of the boat's equipment was not performing properly, including the starboard engine, but in the end all went well and after the lighting of the beacon the Royal Watermen manned the sides of what was now in effect the Royal Barge and we set sail for Greenwich. I was stationed up in the bow, standing at the Jack Stay under the Royal Standard. It was undoubtedly the best possible place to get the full atmosphere of the event and it brought a lump to my throat as we passed the cheering crowds on the riverbanks and the many vessels moored along the route.

As we breasted the glorious looking HMS *Belfast*, dressed overall with her uniformed ratings lining her decks and came up level with her, a guard of honour manning her gangway, they 'Piped the Ship's side' and she lowered her White Ensign in salute to the Royal Barge. As HM Bargemaster I turned slowly to Starboard to face the ship and saluted in return. It was an extremely proud moment.

On arrival at the Dome we disembarked The Queen with the Royal Party and stood-by the Royal Barge in preparation to take Her Majesty across the river to Reuters Pier when the show finished. The Queen had very graciously invited the wives of The Royal Watermen on duty to watch the show from within the Dome, which unfortunately, as the Royal Watermen, we could not see as we stood by guarding the vessel.

When the performance was over and having taken The Queen across the river to Router's Pier, our final duty was to take a boat-load of VIPs back to Westminster. On board were mostly MPs including the Prime Minister. Several of the watermen and I had the rare opportunity to talk to these people who run our country. My impression was that their major effort seemed to be taken up in trying to gain the attention of the people above them on the political ladder. One man in particular was noticeable by the way he was slipping in and out and around the various groups, like a vampire whispering into the ears of the senior politicians. One lady MP was very demanding and quite rude to the Royal Watermen, apparently thinking that they were the crew of the boat. We all gave her a very wide berth. In all in was quite an eye opener to see these people up close and I must say not very inspiring.

In 2002 to honour Her Majesty's Golden Jubilee, the Royal Watermen and I were invited to have a photograph taken with the Queen in the Gold Room at Buckingham Palace. Not only were our wives invited, but all retired Royal Watermen and their wives were also invited. All serving Royal Watermen had been awarded the Golden Jubilee medal by Her Majesty and in return they decided to commission from me a model of the Royal Barge *Nore*, with figurines of the Queen and Duke of Edinburgh with all eight Royal Watermen and Bargemaster on-deck. It was to be gold plated and presented in a glass case.

The day came and on arrival at the palace I received instruction from Colonel Ross on how things were to run. This is typical of palace procedures, most information comes on the day itself, which is in fact a good thing, as it avoids advance worry and concerns, but of course it puts more pressure on the day, particularly on the moments before The Queen comes into the room. My biggest worry was that I might mentally freeze up and forget names when introducing each man and his partner.

The procedure was that the Royal Watermen in office were to assemble in the Gold Room seated ready for the photograph. I was to wait outside with Col Ross to meet and greet Her Majesty, then escort her into the room and to her seat 'Front and Centre' of the assembled watermen. The Queen was her normal relaxed self, making me feel quite at ease. We sat down together and the photographer started to take his shots with the aid of his assistant. When at last the photographs were taken, I proposed to Her Majesty that she might wish to meet all her living watermen and their wives, to which she readily agreed. We progressed into the Green Room which was next door. The first thing was to present the gift of the model MV *Nore*. Her Majesty seemed to be genuinely pleased with the golden model, recalling the many times she had been aboard the vessel.

The men were standing with their partners in a semi-circle, in no particular order and I started to make the introductions starting at the far left, the third man in was Robert Prentice and his wife. The Queen shook hands and said a few words then moved on to the other men, shaking hands with men and wives and making small talk. There were about seventy people in the semi-circle and as we approached the last few over on the right side, almost the last one to be introduced was Paul Prentice and his wife. As I made the introduction, The Queen suddenly astonished me

HM The Queen with her Bargemaster and Watermen in the Gold Room of Buckingham Palace in 2002. (Picture by J. Borg Photography)

by saying 'Oh! Another Mr. Prentice'. I could not believe that without any pre-knowledge of the names or positions, she had remembered that she had been introduced to Paul's brother Robert at the beginning of the group. This was yet another example of Her Majesty's extraordinary ability to remember and assimilate information.

All good things eventually come to an end and the final year of my time as HM Bargemaster arrived in 2002. I should have finished in May of 2002, but the Palace Comptroller had asked me to stay in office to the end of the year for Her Majesty's Golden Jubilee celebrations. My time as Royal Bargemaster was finally over, leaving me with a store of wonderful memories to cherish for the rest of my days, and yet the best was still to come. I received a letter through the post offering me a very special honour, one that is only in the gift of The Queen. I was invited to become a member of The Victorian Order, an MVO.

The day came when with my wife Ursula, my daughter Nathalie and my nephew Jerome we went to Buckingham Palace for the presentation to be made by the Queen. When my turn came to step up before the Sovereign, I came forward and made a bow. She responded by offering me her hand and saying 'I almost did not recognise you without your red uniform'. I smiled but did not reply, feeling a little tongue-tied. She then said. 'I understand that thanks are due to you for staying in office an extra year to organise the river part of the Jubilee celebrations.' I said it had been my pleasure and a great honour to have done so. She then pinned my MVO onto the clip which we had all had positioned on our coats beforehand. I stepped back and bowed again, fully aware that my family were in the audience watching me in my moment of glory. After the presentation as the recipients were all milling around in the Palace forecourt having photographs taken of their great day, I found that my family and I were invited by Col Ross to his room in the Privy Purse office where he and his staff had arranged a small party with champagne and nibbles to celebrate my investiture. Yet another very special acknowledgement.

Looking back over the names of Royal Bargemasters since the time of Edward I, I feel sure those men would all have had a special story to tell. For some it would be a tale of politically turbulent and violent times, for others like me it would have been serving a good Monarch in times of plenty. I feel sure that holding the appointment of Bargemaster must have meant as great an honour to them as it does to us holding the post today.

It has taken some seventy years for me to come through from those days as a 10-year-old helping my Dad with his rowing skiff at Greenwich Buoys and assisting the RAS delivery baker with his horse and cart, to be rubbing shoulders with the highest in the land. A wonderful life indeed, for which I am truly grateful to whoever is watching over me from on high. For a humble Thames waterman, such good fortune can only be said to be awesome.

KENNETH DWAN

HM Bargemaster 2002–04

Kenneth Victor Dwan is a winner of Doggett's Coat and Badge and a former British rower who competed in the Olympic Games in both 1968 and 1972, and also won the Wingfield Sculls on six occasions.

Ken Dwan was born on 6 July 1948 in Rotherhithe, London, to a family of watermen and lightermen of the River Thames in the Port of London.

He joined Poplar, Blackwall and District Rowing Club at the age of 12, initially as a cox, but soon started as an oarsman. When he was 15 he was apprenticed to his grandfather William as a waterman and lighterman of the River Thames, which allowed him to enter the novice sculls in the National Dock Labour Board (NDLB) regatta at Putney.

Above: Gloriana leading the rowing section of the Diamond Jubilee flotilla, 2012. (Malcolm Knight)

Left: HM Bargemaster R. Crouch with Royal Watermen at Hampton Court. (Picture by kind permission of Julian Calder Photography)

Above: Golden model of *Royal Nore* gifted to Her Majesty by her Watermen to commemorate her Golden Jubilee. (Picture taken by model maker R.G. Crouch, HM Bargemaster)

Left: Uniform of HM Bargemaster. Design based on Court dress. (Picture by kind permission of artist Gerald Monlin)

Right: The replica Royal Barge built for the film *A Man For All Seasons* by Turk's of Kingston. (Picture by kind permission of Sue Milton, photographer)

Left: HM Bargemaster carrying the Stela in the Tudor Pull ceremony at Hampton Court, 2018. (Picture by kind permission of Sue Milton, photographer)

Right: Royal Shallop *Jubilant* rowed by Royal Watermen in the Tudor Pull, 2011. (Picture by kind permission of Sue Milton, photographer)

Below: The Tudor Pull Stela being delivered to the Tower of London after being rowed down from Hampton Court in 2018. (Picture by kind permission of John Adams)

The shallop *Jubilant* rowed by Royal Watermen at Hampton Court Bridge. (Picture by kind permission of Sue Milton, photographer)

Jubilant being rowed by a crew of disabled oarsmen at Windsor. (Picture by kind permission of Sue Milton, photographer)

The Stela being delivered to the Tower of London, 2018. (Picture by kind permission of John Adams)

A full crew of eighteen Royal Watermen rowing *Gloriana*. (Picture by kind permission of Sue Milton, photographer)

Shallop *Thamesis*, built on the upper Thames, shown here at the Thames Traditional Boat Festival. (Picture by kind permission of Sue Milton, photographer)

HM Bargemaster R. Crouch on duty with Royal Watermen at the opening of the River and Rowing Museum. (Picture by kind permission of Sue Milton, photographer)

Above: Gloriana rowing past the Tower of London manned by Royal Watermen. (Picture by kind permission of Sue Milton, photographer)

Right: One of the early Tudor Pull ceremonies in 1999 at Hampton Court. The event first started in 1986. (Picture by kind permission of Sue Milton, photographer)

HM Bargemaster Ken Dwan steering the shallop *Jubilant* past the finish line at Henley, rowed by Royal Watermen. (Personal collection of Ken Dwan)

He won the race, which included contestants of that year's Doggett's Coat and Badge Race. While he was sculling he continued working as a lighterman and worked for Humphrey & Grey, starting as a boy in the tug *Sir John*. After two years with Humphrey & Grey he obtained his first working licences and went on the dock labour pool to experience a variety of firms.

During 1967 the decasualisation scheme following Mr Devlin's report was implemented and all dock workers had to be allocated to an employer. Dwan was allocated to FT Everard at Greenhithe, of whom he said, 'The management were very good to me in allowing me time to train. I could not have wished for better employers.'

In 1968, Dwan was runner-up in the Diamond Challenge Sculls at Henley Royal Regatta. He also competed for Great Britain in the single scull in the 1968 Olympics in Mexico. He reached the final and came sixth overall. Also in 1968 he won the Wingfield Sculls for the first time. He won the Wingfield Sculls again in 1969, 1970, 1971 and 1972. In 1972 he competed again for Great Britain in the single scull in the Olympics in Munich, finishing ninth. Dwan was runner-up in the Diamond Challenge Sculls in 1974 and won the Wingfield Sculls for the sixth time in 1975.

Ken Dwan, HM The Queen's Bargemaster, stands at the centre, surrounded by Royal Watermen and the crew of the boat. (Personal collection of Ken Dwan)

During his years at the Olympic Games in 1968 and 1972, Dwan was forced to camp in a tent, not being able to afford the cost of hotel accommodation. A fellow competitor from the USA team could not believe the lack of financial support and befriended him, helping out with providing better conditions. In those days the UK had very strict rules regarding amateurs in sport.

In 1977, Dwan was accepted as one of Her Majesty's Royal Watermen during the Queen's Silver Jubilee year. He continued to work as a lighterman, but with severance at the docks now available, he decided to work for himself and withdrew from lighterage and rowing at the same time.

For a while he worked on the building of the Thames Barrier, and then on pleasure boats on the river. He then went into business with Mr W. Ludgrove and they set up their own company, Thames Cruises. The business grew and they bought a repair yard at Eel Pie Island.

Thames Cruises owned the pleasure boat *Marchioness*, which was sunk with loss of life when the pleasure boat was run down from behind by the dredger *Bowbelle* in August 1989. The disaster was found by the Marine Accident Investigation Branch to have been caused by the poor visibility from each vessel's wheelhouse, the fact that both vessels were using the centre of the river and that no clear instructions were given to the lookout at the bow of the *Bowbelle*. Twelve years later, another report by Lord Clarke also blamed poor lookouts on both vessels for the collision and criticised the owners and managers of both vessels for failing to properly instruct and monitor their crews.

The pleasureboat *Hurlingham* which was also owned by Dwan's company was nearby to the *Marchioness* on that dreadful night, and was able to rescue some fifty-two people from the river, a fact not often reported.

In 2002, Ken Dwan was appointed the Queen's Bargemaster, chosen from among the serving Royal Watermen to replace the retiring Bob Crouch, being responsible for organising their duties and for the safety of the Queen when she travelled by water. However, in light of protests from members of the public because of his boat company's involvement with the *Bowbelle/Marchioness* disaster, he decided to step down as HM Bargemaster so as to avoid any embarrassment to Her Majesty or to his office, in itself a demonstration of his loyalty to the Crown.

PAUL LUDWIG

HM Bargemaster 2003–17

River Reminisces by Paul Ludwig

My earliest memory of the River Thames was at 8 years old when my eldest brother Michael took me to work with him at Montague L. Mayer's yard at Rainham in Kent where I recall he had to uncover a cargo barge. From that moment I fell in love with the river and decided when I grew up I wanted to be a Lighterman.

My career on the Thames started with the towing firm of Gaselee and Son in 1963 working aboard the tug *Naja*. If I'd known at the time the history of her predecessor which took a direct hit by a V1 bomb in 1944 killing all six crew, I may have thought twice about working aboard her. To confirm my superstitions one of the stays on the engine room skylight was broken which resulted in it slamming down on my left hand, damaging the joint of my third finger, I still have the scars. At the time I thought it was good of Gaselee to pay me for the time I was off work!

HM Bargemaster Paul Ludwig at the helm of the Queen's Row-Barge *Gloriana* at Hampton Court Palace, about to leave and head off for the Tudor Pull bound for the Tower of London in 2016. (Picture by Reflections Photography)

Later on during my time on the *Naja* at about two o'clock one morning a police boat came alongside us. The copper in charge asked my skipper if he would run the tug down river to the buoy above Regents Canal Dock (Paddy's Buoy) where a barge loaded with reels of printing paper had sunk. He wanted us to tow the remaining craft, now hanging on the buoy, over to King and Queen. We did go down and have a look, it was pouring down with rain and very dark, there was only the skipper and engineer aboard the tug. Fortunately my skipper decided it was too dangerous … phew!

On another occasion at about midnight we were alongside Union Lighterage's craft at Butlers Wharf when one of the crew aboard *Royal Daffodil* which was moored on Georges Stairs Tier fell over the side. It was flood tide and at the time I had my head down in the aft cabin. The skipper came along the deck and called down the hatch for me to get on deck, being 15 years old I didn't respond until he came along the second time. By then the crew member in the water was more or less abreast of us. Our skipper let the tug fall away from the moored craft and we started to go slowly astern towards Tower Bridge. I was standing by on the aft deck with the tug's hitcher, the water was like glass with the reflection of the light off of the bridge. As we drew near to the bridge-arch you could see the swell off the abutment like a slow bow wave, but sadly as we drew nearer the eddy drew the crew member under the water and we never saw him again. The memory of that night remained with me for a very long while thinking that if I'd have got up the first time the skipper called me he might have survived.

I began working in pleasure boats in 1965 aboard a boat called the *Viking III* with an old tug skipper by the name of Bill Squires. He was quite a character, and very partial to Dimple Haig whisky. At times, if we were the light boat up from Greenwich and the tide was right, we would go alongside the ladder at the 'Mayflower' in Rotherhithe where he would have a swift one!

During my time in pleasure boats I was fortunate to be with a forward looking firm run by Alan Woods who built several boats over the thirty-nine years I was working there. On several occasions aboard different vessels I was fortunate to be close to and indeed meet some very famous people including in 1972 the Prince of Wales who had hired *Silver Dolphin* for a lunch with his Buckingham Palace staff. I was also aboard *Silver Marlin* when there was a reception for Neil Armstrong when he visited the UK after becoming the first person to walk on the moon in 1969. Once when I found myself behind the bar on *Silver Marlin* I refused Michael Caine a cup of coffee (we didn't have any cups) – 'not a lot of people know that'. The list goes on.

I was appointed a Waterman to the Queen in 1993. One of my first duties was the State Opening of Parliament. On the day, the Bargemaster and Watermen met in a café in Crown Passage which is quite close to St James's Palace where our uniforms are kept. After tea and a bacon roll we made our way over to the Palace and were let in by the Superintendent of the State Apartments via Friary Court Door. Entering the palace is quite surreal when you are surrounded by massive paintings of past British monarchs and other historical artefacts. We made our way along the hallway and up the stairs to the room where our uniforms are stored. After an hour or so, our transport arrived and we were taken over to the Royal Mews at Buckingham Palace where the carriages and horses were being prepared for the State Opening. The whole day was incredible and quite unbelievable and I certainly was honoured to be part of it.

I was fortunate to become Bargemaster to Her Majesty the Queen in 2003. The State Opening of Parliament was again my first duty. As Royal Bargemaster I had the privilege of receiving the Imperial State Crown from the Comptroller of the Lord Chamberlain's Office as part of loading the regalia aboard the carriage.

To date I have attended 13 State Openings of Parliament and many more State Visits. In my time as Bargemaster I have been fortunate to be in office for many special occasions including the Diamond Jubilee Pageant held on the Thames in 2012.

The Watermen were fortunate to be allowed to have their photograph taken with Her Majesty in recognition of her sixty years as monarch; this was at Buckingham Palace in 2013 and again when Her Majesty visited Watermen's Hall in March 2014.

On another occasion the Watermen were in attendance to Her Majesty when she came aboard the Queen's Row Barge *Gloriana* at Windsor for a tea cruise. This was the first time the monarch had been rowed on the Thames by the Royal Watermen since the Peace Pageant in 1919. Her Majesty came aboard in the grounds of Windsor Castle along with Prince Andrew, Prince Edward and the Countess of Wessex.

In 2011 I was elected Master of The Company of Watermen and Lightermen of the River Thames. During the year I was Master I visited

Paul Ludwig at Hampton Court in September 2016, collecting the Thames River Stela for the annual Tudor Pull to be rowed to the Tower of London. (Picture by Reflections Photography)

many other livery halls in the City of London for lunch or dinner, always with a warm welcome from the Master or Prime Warden and other Freemen and Liverymen. The office of Master carries with it great responsibility which cannot be carried out successfully without having a good team of Officers of the Company and Wardens behind you, which I was fortunate to have. My term in office overlapped into the 2012 celebrations for the Diamond Jubilee, so at the time of the Diamond Jubilee Pageant when standing at the head of the *Spirit of Chartwell* with Her Majesty on board and most of the other members of the Royal family I was both Bargemaster to Her Majesty the Queen and Master of The Company of Watermen and Lightermen.

CHRISTOPHER LIVETT

HM Bargemaster, appointed 2017

I was born into a River Thames family as a seventh generation Waterman and Lighterman. My early years were spent on board tugs with my father; these had names like the *Arthur Darling*, *Fossa*, *Sandtex* and *Cullex*. I remember being passed from one tug to another and also being sent to different locations, one day in Brentford, the next being in Holehaven Creek, which gave me an early understanding of the geography and the different parts of the Thames.

Even at this tender age, I was involved with the towing of small ships of some 3,000 gross tonnage, helping to bring them of out of Deptford Creek with the 180 hp tug called *Scoundrel*. This was not a job for the faint hearted. My early helter-skelter life is perhaps best indicted by the fact that I left school aged 16 on a Friday and was at sea as a young seaman the following Monday, not to come home for some nine months.

My sporting life started when I learnt to row at the Globe Rowing Club, Greenwich under the watchful eye of Ray Easterling, a very good coach and a Doggett's Coat and Badge winner. Globe RC had a floating boathouse (a converted Thames lighter). The heavy clinker boats were stored in this barge afloat, with the heavier eights which were in two sections having to be coupled together before each outing; this was after we had negotiated the enormous flood gate at the Highbridge Draw dock which it seemed had only one mission in its life, to take our fingers off!

I was apprenticed to my father as my master to learn my trade as a waterman and lighterman and I worked in most aspects of river life including passenger boats, lighterage, bunkering, civil engineering and ship mooring, which gave me a very good grounding for my future on the tideway. During this time I was also committed to training for my chance to row for Doggett's Coat and Badge.

My race for the Coat in 1982 was one of the first years for quite some time when, because more than six men were eligible to row, heats were undertaken from Hammersmith to Putney. It also turned out to be an extremely close and competitive event. It was eventful for several reasons: one competitor, Mr Winn, in trying to use the tide flow to his advantage rowed into the barge moorings at Coin Street near Blackfriars and having gone athwart of the mooring chain and under the swim of the barge, his boat was broken up and he was washed down under the full length of the barge. He was very fortunate to be pulled out the other end as he surfaced by the author of this book who was manning the nearby safety boat.

Another competitor in the race, Gary Ennis, and I were closely matched in the lead, sculling level with each other when just before Westminster Bridge the umpire alerted us to an outward bound ship the *Bowbelle*, a suction dredger of considerable size which was making its way down over the course, despite the fact the river should have been closed. Both Gary and I took avoiding action – Gary choosing to go north and me diving south. The north shore was the quickest and shortest route and gave Gary the chance of taking and holding this advantage which lead to him going on to win his well-deserved Coat and Badge.

Having worked in the passenger boat industry during my apprenticeship and taking command of my first passenger boat aged 18, I felt that there was a gap in the market and I decided it was time to take on a new venture in waste disposal, and so began Tidy Thames Refuse Services.

Whilst refurbishing my first vessel the *Hooligan* at Greenwich Pier, I met Belinda, the beautiful daughter of an Attendance Waterman. Our meeting took place over a cup of coffee and a Mars bar in a local cafe. Belinda and I fell in love and so began our thirty-four years (and counting) partnership in life and also in business. Sitting knee to knee beneath a desk on Greenwich Pier together, we developed Tidy Thames Refuse Services, the Port's only dedicated refuse service, to the point when we were servicing most Thames passenger boats for their owner/operators. We then expanded the service to include a recycling service which was way ahead of the curve at that time. The service was twice recognised in The Queen Mother's Birthday Awards, which was a huge achievement for us.

With my brother Steven, we then went on to create Livett's Launches, having purchased the MV *Brunel* from the Wilson family and taking over the Tower Pier to HMS *Belfast* ferry service. As planned, this was just the start and over the past thirty years Livett's has expanded its portfolio of craft & services to where today, we are hugely proud to be able say we have worked on a myriad of films and special events featuring the River Thames, to include the James Bond films *The World is Not Enough* and *Spectre*, *Harry Potter* and *The Man from UNCLE* to name but a few, and some of the most iconic marine civil engineering projects.

Having been an apprentice Waterman and Lighterman, a journeyman freeman, craft-owning freeman within the Watermen's Guild, I then joined the Court of the Company in 1990, serving on various committees including Chairmanship of the then Apprentice and Licensing Committee. An offshoot of this which I helped to start with Bob Crouch, Maldwyn Drummond (Fishmongers Company) and both Clerks from Fishmongers and Watermans, was the Thames Traditional Rowing Association and the birth of the Thames Cutters. In 1998 I

Christopher Livett, HM Bargemaster. In 2018 he was Her Majesty's sixth appointed Bargemaster. (Picture by Reflections Photography)

was honoured to become probably the youngest Master of any City Company at the right side of 40 years old.

Having been appointed a Royal Waterman in 2002, I felt this was a great honour and privilege to join this unique, historic and honourable group of first class Watermen serving Her Majesty The Queen.

It was a particular pleasure assisting and being part of the organising committee for the highly successful Diamond Jubilee Pageant in 2012 alongside the Pageant Master Adrian Evans. As a thank you for my contributions, Her Majesty invited me on board the *Spirit of Chartwell* with the

HM Bargemaster C. Livett presenting the Tudor Pull Stela at the Tower of London in 2018. (Picture by kind permission of John Adams)

Royal Family and other dignitaries to view the pageant and experience what would be the highlight of my experiences afloat to date.

Today the Livett Group consists of four businesses – Livett's Launches, Thames Luxury Charters, Bennett's Barges (Tugs and Barges) and Imperial Wharf Marina Ltd, based at Butlers Wharf in the shadow of Tower Bridge. We are still very much a family business, with Belinda my wife and now our son Edward on the bridge of the business steering a steady course. With a fleet of over 30 vessels of one shape or another and employing up to 100 people we are set well for the coming years ahead.

In 2015 I was delighted to become a Liveryman of the Worshipful Company of Shipwrights and support the Shipwrights Company in its charitable aims and objectives in relation to apprentice training in the maritime world. Having been a Trustee of the *Cutty Sark* for seven years and seeing her reborn from a dilapidated museum piece into a stunning first class global attraction was very satisfying and demonstrated the ship-wrights' skills that still exist within the UK. This, despite a mammoth fund-raising challenge and the awful fire, was a huge achievement by all concerned, under the watchful eye of the Duke of Edinburgh, President of the Cutty Sark Trust, and the past Chairmanship of the late Maurice De Rohan and later Lord Sterling of Plaistow.

In 2017 I was honoured to be accepted as a Younger Brother of Trinity House. This ancient Fraternity which is the same age as the Waterman's Company is not only responsible for the navigation lights and aids in UK waters, but is also a major contributor to the UK maritime charities assisting a broad range of people in maritime training and other activities. As the past Chairman of the Thames Training Alliance and currently a Board member of the Thames Skills Academy, I am keen to see the Inland Waterways of the UK are well represented and assist in the aims and objectives of Trinity House establishing a structured, funded path way for young and old into maritime employment, whether this be on inland waters or offshore.

Following an interview at Buckingham Palace in November 2017, I received a very special communication to say that Her Majesty The Queen had approved the recommendation of the interview panel to appoint me as Her Majesty's Bargemaster. This is the pinnacle of my life afloat and it was with enormous pleasure that I happily accepted the post. To be 'The Queen's Man on the River' is a very special appointment and I very much look forward to working with the team at Buckingham Palace and our distinguished Royal Watermen in serving Her Majesty and other members of the Royal Family afloat on the Royal River Thames. To become Her Majesty's sixth Bargemaster during her long reign and to follow in the footsteps of the highly respected, experienced and esteemed predecessors will be a tough act to follow, but I am determined to keep up the traditions, maintain standards and promote from our privileged positions to the benefit of others in matters relating to our Queen and the River Thames.

Today's Royal Bargemasters

Today's Royal Bargemaster and Watermen retire at the age of 65. On the retirement of a Royal Waterman, a replacement must be found. A new man is obtained from the list of qualified men who have offered their service and are young enough to be able to serve ten to fifteen years of appointment to Her Majesty. The Bargemaster will shortlist those most suitably qualified and arrange for their interview by the Palace Comptroller at the Privy Purse Office in Buckingham Palace.

It is interesting to note that only men working as watermen or boat-builders can become Royal Watermen. Boatbuilders have for centuries had a special relationship with the watermen's trade, and were allowed by the Watermen's Guild to manoeuvre vessels in and out of their boatbuilding yard as this required a special skill of working with the tidal regime to place vessels onto the working grids and slipways of the yard.

A man lucky enough to be chosen will receive his appointment document signed by the Queen and will be called for duty by HM Bargemaster for river or road carriage duties throughout the term of his appointment.

The honour of becoming a Royal Waterman, although unpaid, is much sought after among the river fraternity. Like many of England's traditions, it seems at first glance to be outdated, but on closer examination the merit of this convention becomes more evident. Men from humble backgrounds find themselves involved with other levels of British society, leading to a better understanding of how the British system works. The Royal Watermen see themselves supporting this country's unrivalled structure of an elected government with the continuance and stability of the monarchy.

Today, a new Royal Bargemaster is selected by recommendation from the retiring Bargemaster of appropriate candidates from among the ranks of the serving Royal Watermen. At age of retirement, the retiring Bargemaster is

Royal Shallop *Jubilant* being launched at Richmond. (Picture by R. Mutton, Jubilant Trust)

requested by the Palace Comptroller, acting for Her Majesty, to produce a shortlist of serving Royal Watermen whom he feels would be suitable to replace him. This shortlist is used to interview the candidates, who are called for the purpose to the Privy Purse office at Buckingham Palace. Each interview is attended by the Comptroller, his assistant, the Bargemaster and a secretary. The outcome of each interview is discussed and after all interviews are completed, a likely candidate is chosen. The Comptroller then advises Her Majesty as to the suggested choice of her new Bargemaster.

If Her Majesty approves the choice, a letter is then sent on behalf of the Queen to the candidate offering him the appointment as Her Majesty's personal Bargemaster. On written acceptance, a formal warrant is issued and from that moment the new man is in post.

Royal Watermen Rowing on the Thames

The outgoing Bargemaster will assist with the arrangements for the fitting of a new man's uniform and regalia. He will also pass over the lists of Royal Watermen in post, with telephone numbers and addresses, along with any paperwork for upcoming duties.

Royal Watermen under the command of HM Bargemaster rowing past the Syon estate at Isleworth in the 2007 Tudor Pull. (Picture by Reflections Photography)

V

THE ROYAL FAMILY
AFLOAT

Members of today's Royal Family have used numerous vessels as a Royal Barge for various river duties over recent years, reinforcing the importance of the Thames as a show-place as well as the water artery of London. Because Her Majesty's Bargemaster and Watermen are personal appointments to the monarch, other members of the Royal Family need the Queen's permission for their use.

Gloriana being rowed on the Thames through London in 2018. Royal Watermen are under command of HM Bargemaster. (Picture by kind permission of John Adams)

HRH Prince Charles

It was Prince Charles who made the suggestion of a waterborne tribute to celebrate his mother's Diamond Jubilee, and as patron of the event he oversaw the river flotilla as it passed along the Thames.

One of the most impressive vessels in the pageant was *Gloriana*. The newly built replica state row-barge led the oar-powered section of the parade, being rowed by Olympic gold medallists Sir Steve Redgrave and Sir Matthew Pinsent with sixteen others.

Havengore, the vessel that carried Sir Winston Churchill's coffin during his state funeral in 1965, was used in the pageant by the Duke of York and his family, along with the Earl and Countess of Wessex. The Princess Royal and her husband, Vice Admiral Sir Timothy Laurence, were on board the *Trinity House* vessel.

The temporary Royal Barge *Sprite of Chartwell* was lavishly decorated with carvings in a red, gold and purple colour scheme, the vessel's design echoing the highly ornate royal barges of the seventeenth and eighteenth centuries. The pageant organisers succeeded in recreating a parade not seen on the river for more than 300 years, since the reign of Charles II.

Members of Royal Family aboard the Queen's Row-Barge for BBC Children awards. (Picture by Sue Milton, photographer)

The Queen, accompanied by her Bargemaster and Watermen aboard the *Sprite of Chartwell*, was escorted down the river by a 1,000-strong flotilla to mark her sixty-year reign. She was joined on this opulently decorated barge by the Duke of Edinburgh, Prince of Wales, Duchess of Cornwall, Duke and Duchess of Cambridge and Prince Harry. Her Majesty was cheered all the way by the enormous crowds manning both sides of the river, in a show of true affection for their monarch, displaying the popular acceptance of the British system of constitutional monarchy.

The broadcaster Andrew Marr in his BBC show, speaking about the monarchy, hit the appropriate chord when he commented that there would be less stability in Britain if the Royal Family did not exist. He said:

> I think one of the great things that a monarch brings, and particularly a Royal Family and Her Majesty the Queen personally brings, is this sense of national unity and stability, someone who the whole country can identify with, it doesn't matter whether people are Labour or Conservative or Liberal Democrat or can't bear any politicians. There at the head of state is someone who the whole country can revere and look up to, a great symbol of national unity, of continuity, that links British people with our institutions, with our history, with our relations with other countries, with the Commonwealth. All of those things help to anchor us, so I think it's a great source of strength and stability, both now and into the future. And you get the sense with her that she will go on doing the amazing job she's done for this country as long as she possibly can and you never see any sign of her devotion getting any less.

HRH Princess Anne

The Princess Royal has recently taken over from Prince Philip, the Duke of Edinburgh, as Master of the Fishmongers' Company, who are the organisers of the Doggett's Coat and Badge Wager, the watermen's premier rowing event. This will give her another link to the Thames through this famous race, which was started by Doggett to honour the first of the Hanoverian kings, George I.

In 1714, the Irish actor Thomas Doggett provided money to endow a boat race called the Hanoverian Wager in honour of the new king. The race was originally to be rowed annually in August by up to six young watermen who were to be just out of their apprenticeship. The prize for the race was to be a orange-red coat with a silver arm badge depicting the white horse of Hanover. Since Doggett's death, the Fishmongers' Company continues to organise this event each year; it is now believed to be the world's longest continuously held sporting event, the oldest boat race in the world and is 4 miles and 5 furlongs long.

HRH Prince Andrew

On 14 September 2002, Prince Andrew launched the Royal Shallop *Jubilant* for 'The Celebration of Time', an event to celebrate the Queen's Golden Jubilee and to introduce this newly built replica shallop to the Thames.

Jubilant was rowed by Royal Watermen under the command of HM Bargemaster and carried 'Time', in the form of an atomic clock, from the old observatory at Kew to the observatory at Greenwich. The shallop was accompanied by a floatier of cutters owned by City Livery Companies.

Jubilant was built by Mark Edwards at Richmond-on-Thames in 1995 to promote traditional, fixed-seat rowing and help publicise this new code of rowing. It is now used for training disabled rowers, enabling them to join able-bodied rowers in river events, ceremonies and regattas on the Thames. *Jubilant* has been a regular feature on the tidal Thames in events and celebrations. It is possibly the best design of the vessel type of an oared

Prince Andrew pouring a bottle of champagne over the bow of *Jubilant* before its trip from Kew to Greenwich in 2002. (Picture by R. Mutton, Jubilant Trust)

Royal Barge, but although rowed many times by the Royal Watermen, it has never been the official Royal Barge.

HRH Prince Edward

In 1991, Prince Edward was filmed for a documentary aboard the *Lady Mayoress* shallop while being rowed by watermen from Tower pier to Westminster. He travelled with Her Majesty's Bargemaster Robert Crouch, who after the event said he was very impressed by the Prince's knowledge of the history of the Thames and that of the Royal Watermen.

Lady Mayoress was built at the request of the Company of Watermen and Lightermen of the River Thames, and is a 42ft shallop barge, but without a permanent cabin; instead it has a collapsible 'Tilt' at the stern. Shown being rowed by six rowers, plus a coxswain, it can carry up to four passengers. *Lady Mayoress* is another of the Richmond-built boats, and is also used regularly in river events.

Of the many memorable stories concerning the use of Royal Barges, an incident in 1256 involving Queen Eleanor of Castile when she was involved in an incident at London Bridge is worth retelling. The populace, who were against the Queen, hurled rotten vegetables and rocks in an effort to capsize her barge as it was attempting to shoot under the bridge arch, but they did not succeed. Her Bargemaster managed to get the barge back to shore, where she was then rescued by the Mayor of London and helped back to the Tower. If the barge had passed through the bridge it would probably have been sunk on the other side of the arch. The Bargemaster, realising this danger, got the barge back to shore without completing the shoot under the bridge. It would seem that Queen Eleanor's life was saved by the skill of her Royal Bargemaster and the Royal Watermen.

Each year, Her Majesty's Watermen complete a marathon row, called the Tudor Pull, from Hampton Court Palace to the Tower of London, a distance of some 25 miles, to deliver under oars a stela (upright tablet) representing the water of London's river. They do this to demonstrate their continuing ability to match the rowing capability of their forefathers, to support the apprentices system of their trade and to draw attention to London's great under-used asset, the River Thames.

HRH Prince Edward with HM Bargemaster in the shallop *Lady Mayoress*, steered by the Watermen's Co. Bargemaster. (Picture by kind permission of HRH Prince Edward's Office)

HRH Prince Edward filmed on the Thames in the shallop barge *Lady Mayoress* being rowed to Westminster. (Picture by kind permission of HRH Prince Edward's Office)

State Row-Barge Gloriana

The eighteen-oared *Gloriana* is the most recent row-vessel to be built. It is a full-size replica of a City Livery Company Barge and can carry up to twenty passengers. Not as fast or manoeuvrable as the eight-oared shallops historically used by royalty, this type of vessel is built for show and display.

Gloriana also took part in the rowing section of the Diamond Jubilee pageant, which took place in 2012 and included military, commercial and pleasure craft.

The river pageant was a great success, despite the unseasonably wet weather. According to Guinness World Records, it was the largest ever parade of boats on an inland waterway, surpassing the previous record of 327 vessels set in Bremerhaven, Germany, in 2011.

Gloriana at Windsor Home Park with the Royal Family aboard, rowed by eighteen Watermen under HM Bargemaster Paul Ludwig. (Picture by Malcolm Knight, Gloriana Trust)

The Queen and Duke of Edinburgh happily watching a procession from Chelsea Pier. (Picture by Sue Milton, photographer)

VI

APPOINTMENTS, UNIFORMS AND WAGES

Appointment

In the past the appointment of the Master of the Barge could be for life, but sometimes the office was held only during good behaviour. When a new monarch took the throne, the Royal Bargemaster(s) and Royal Watermen were sometimes readmitted. This readmission could and did cause confusion, especially when made during a time when a particular family, such as the Warners of Greenwich, were Royal Bargemasters through several generations.

Some records of appointment are a gold mine of information. A good example of this is the document appointing Thomas Coxe in 1554, which quotes within it who his five predecessors were: '[T]he office of master of the Queen's barges and the boats, which office John Bundye deceased, lately held, with the wages and fees To hold the office as fully as Bundye or Thomas Ragge, John Carter, John Johnson, John Thruston or any other person held it.'[1]

The wording of their appointment/reappointment was often similar over the centuries, as can be seen by the following entries. In 1685, the warrant requiring the Gentleman Usher in Daily Waiting to admit Daniell Hill as Master of the Barges reads as follows: 'This is to require you to swear and admit Mr Daniell Hill in the place and quality of Master of the Barges in Ordinary to His Majestie King James the Second To enjoy the said place with all rights profits privileges and advantages thereto belonging.'[2]

In 1760, when John Mason was appointed/reappointed, the wording was as follows: '[S]worn and admitted John Mason into the place and quality of

Barge Master in Ordinary to His Majesty to hold Exercise and Enjoy the said place together with all Rights Profites Privileges and Advantages there unto belonging. In full and Ample manner as any Master of The Barges formerly Held and Enjoyed the same.' This appointment was given under the hand and seal of William Fitzherbert, Gentleman Usher, Daily Waiter, on 17 December 1760.[3]

Uniform

Generally, records show that the Bargemaster and the Royal Watermen had similar standards of livery. On occasion, however, the Bargemaster had the superior standard of Court livery.

The Royal Bargemaster dealt with the practicalities of organising the uniforms for himself and the Royal Watermen under his command. This seems to be the case from as far back as the reign of Edward IV.

The issue of livery for the Master of the Barges (presumably also the Deputy) and the Royal Watermen took place very regularly. New livery was also granted for special occasions such as coronations and royal funerals. New livery for coronations was usually scarlet, while that for royal funerals was naturally black. It seems customary that the Royal Bargemaster and his Royal Watermen were granted new livery for mourning purposes, but it is not always clear whether they actually took part in their late monarch's funeral. Throughout history, periods of mourning were observed when a monarch died, which could vary from weeks to months and even up to a year. If the Court was observing mourning, then the Royal Bargemaster would be in mourning livery for the same period of time.

On 24 July 1480, a 'gown of black camlet' was delivered to the Master of the King's Barge 'against the Duchess coming', this relating to the visit of the King's sister, Margaret, Duchess of Burgundy. The Bargemaster and his twenty-four Watermen also received 16 yards of blue and murrey cloth (Yorkist colours) to make jackets and forty-eight small roses to garnish them. The implication is that the gown of black camlet was issued as a mark of the Master's rank within the Court at that time.[4]

The style of the Royal Bargemaster's uniform of today suggests it may be of late Georgian origin, whereas that of the Royal Watermen has a Tudor look to it.

This suggestion is borne out by the yardage issued to the Royal Bargemaster and the Royal Waterman, which, certainly in Queen Anne's time was similar. This suggests the style and cut were similar. For example, when they were issued with black livery for the funeral of Queen Anne in August 1714, there was a warrant issued by the Lord Chamberlain's department as follows:

> For nine yards of superfine black cloth and six yards of black bays. One hundred and fifty six yards of fine black cloth and one hundred and forty four yards of black bays for the Master of the Barges and forty-eight watermen.
>
> For two pairs of very fine Worsted stockings and forty eight pairs of large black Woosted [worsted] stockings for the Master of the Barges and forty eight watermen plus four gross of silk points [these were silk cords with metal points at each end – used for fastening the uniform].

The warrant also serves to demonstrate that at this time the Royal Bargemaster was issued with a higher quality of material for his uniform than that of his Watermen.[5]

A further warrant is issued requesting delivery to Mr Christopher Hill, Master of His Majesty's Barges, of mourning liveries for himself and forty-eight Watermen, dated 12 August 1714, the first year of George I's reign.[6]

As has been demonstrated by the amount of cloth used in the making of the Bargemaster's and Watermen's uniform, it would seem that they were probably of a similar cut until the nineteenth century. One possibility is that the Bargemaster's uniform changed when George IV introduced a Court uniform based on the 'Windsor Uniform' in 1820. The Court uniform consisted of tail coat and breeches. Perhaps the Watermen retained their more voluminous uniforms to take into account that they were doing a very physical job, and that a tail coat and breeches would have been too tight-fitting to be compatible with such work. Another possibility is that the Bargemaster may have been required to attend Court, and thus it was thought appropriate that he wore a variation of the new Court uniform.

As to the colour of the uniform, it is likewise difficult to be specific as to when it became scarlet on a permanent basis. Generally, the best evidence comes from documents relating to the expenditure of the Royal household. Expenditure on uniforms usually specifies the yardage and its cost, but not

always its colour. Just to make matters more confusing, scarlet would sometimes be used for special occasions such as coronations, when the entire
household would be resplendent in new red uniforms.

In medieval times, it would appear that the livery colours of the monarch
were used, such as murrey and blue, the Yorkist colours.

When we reach the Tudor period, the subject of colour becomes more
blurred. Henry VIII used his livery colours of green and white frequently,
particularly for barge cloths (see the chapter on barges).

The following warrants and descriptions of uniforms for the Guard,
Halberdiers and Archers demonstrate that nothing was set in stone with
regard to uniform colours at this time:

> 31st October 1511. Warrant to the Great Wardrobe. Enough green and
> white cloth for 100 jackets for the guard.
>
> 6th November 1516. Warrant for red wool coats were ordered for 120
> yeomen of the guard.
>
> 7th June 1520. After the ladies came all the bodyguard, namely 200
> archers; one half bowmen and the other half halberdiers, with doublets of
> green velvet and white satin.

Although these warrants relate to Henry's Guard, they are probably indica-
tive that during this period, the colours of the Royal Bargemasters' uniforms
may also have been subject to change.

I suspect that the red uniforms may have become standard during the
reign of Elizabeth I, as is suggested by the following quotation: 'The Lady
Elizabeth, however, did not give green and white to her own men. Her
livery was scarlet or fine red, guarded with black velvet.'[7]

According to a letter dated 1 July 1685, the Master of the Barges was given
6 yards of bastard scarlet at 26s per yard and 6 yards of bayse at 2s 8d per yard.
There was also four gross of silk points at 4s a dozen, 14 ells (an ell measured
about 45in) of Holland at 7s an ell and a velvet cap. In the same letter, the
Watermen received 1¾ yards of bastard scarlet at 15s a yard.[8]

On 10th November 1690, a warrant was issued to the Rt Hon the
Earle of Montagu, Master of His Majesty's Great Wardrobe, regarding their
uniforms: 'These are to signifie unto your Lordship His Majesty's pleasure that you provide and deliver unto John Warner, Esquire, Master of His
Majesty's Barges for Liverys … for each of them the said watermen one yard

three quarters of Bastard Scarlett at fifteen shillings the yard.' He was also to supply Mr Warner with 3 yards of lining for the same at 2*s* 8*d* per yard and one velvet cap each.[9]

Sometimes records even tell us who supplied items of livery: 'David Bosanquet, merchant, bonnets of black Genoa velvet for Bargemaster and Watermen of The Queen and of her late Consort, Prince George of Denmark.'[10]

John Bee, hosier, supplied several pairs of hose for the Bargemasters and Watermen. Bee seems to have been a shoemaker too: 'John Bee, shoemaker, for several pairs of shoes for the 140 Yeomen and Yeoman Warders, for the Queen's Bargemaster and 58 Watermen of the Queen's and of the late Prince's barges, for the 10 children of the Chapel Royal, and for the 50 poor men of the Royal Maundy £76.'[11]

In 1717, John Robinson, linen draper, was paid for 'Holland, cambric and cotton for the King's Majesty, for the Children of the Chapel Royal, for the King's Bargemaster and for the watermen'. This was presumably for shirts.[12]

Ordinary livery, certainly during some periods in history, was granted on a yearly basis, as is seen from the following warrant:

September 25th 1729

    Order from the Lords of the Treasury confirming a warrant from the Duke of Grafton to the Duke of Montagu, of date 1729, September 13, for the provision and delivery to Robert Mason, master of His Majesty's barges, of liveries for himself and 48 watermen for 1729, and for 12 pensionary watermen.

There is also a Memorandum which gives the cost of the livery as £342 or thereabouts.[13] A similar warrant was also granted on 29 September 1730 for liveries for that year.

The following is a description of the Royal Watermen's uniform in the time of Edward VII:

COAT – Scarlet Regulation Watermen's shape, with full skirts. Scarlet collar with Blue Velvet patches in front with one small button. Small three point slash on sleeve with five small Gilt buttons. Silver Badge of special design on front and back, fastened on by seventeen large Gilt buttons in front and sewn on at back. Lined Blue Serge.
BUTTONS – Royal Cypher and Crown.

BREECHES – Scarlet Cloth, split falls, four small Gilt buttons at knees.
HAT – Velvet Hunting Cap.
STOCKINGS – Scarlet.
SHOES – Black Calf, laced.
GLOVES – White Cotton

Unfortunately no mention is made of the Royal Bargemaster's uniform of this time.[14]

There is a painting at Watermen's Hall of Reginald Frances, one of the Rulers of the Company, who was also a Royal Waterman. There is a story passed down within the company that he had been given cloth by the then Royal Bargemaster to have made up into a new uniform. However, he decided that his old uniform was still in good enough condition, so had the cloth turned into curtains for his office. There is no evidence of him having been punished for this.

Badges

There has long been a tradition of the Royal Bargemaster and his Watermen being issued with silver badges denoting their office.

During the Interregnum, Cromwell ordered badges for the State Watermen. On 9 March 1657 a Warrant of the Protector and Council for Payment of Money appears 'to Edward Blackwell, Goldsmith of London For 58 badges for his Highnesses watermen on 2 Orders of Council – £347 6s 5d'. It sounds odd to refer to Oliver Cromwell as His Highness.[15]

When William and Mary ascended the throne in 1689, new badges were ordered. On 21 May 1689, a Treasury Order was issued:

[F]or the execution of a warrant dated May 16 inst, from the Earl of Dorset to the Master of the Jewel House to prepare and deliver to John Warner, master of the King's barges, 49 pairs of badges of silver gilt for himself and 48 watermen: same to be of the same weight as formerly: each pair of badges not to exceed the weight of 50 ounces.

The document goes on to describe the new badges – 'to be made of the following fashion viz the Rose and Crown gilt … with the letters W and R on each side the Rose and Crown, to be worn upon the breast and upon the back of the liveries of the said watermen'.[16]

In 1702, the year that Queen Anne ascended the throne, a Lord Chamberlain's warrant in the Calendar of Treasury Books refers to a 'warrant dated 21st October to the Master of the Jewel House for the delivery to John Warner, Master of Her Majesty's Great Barges, of 48 pairs of silver badges for the watermen's liveries not exceeding 50 ounces each pair and one pair of 60 ounces for the Master'.[17]

After the Act of Union, the Royal Bargemaster and the Royal Watermen had to have new badges which depicted 'with the alteration appointed upon account of the Union with Scotland'.

On 14 June 1708, the Queen's Watermen petitioned the officers of the Jewel Office because the Jewel Office had required them to return their old badges once the new ones were issued. They wished to keep them, 'having no other perquisites'.[18]

Later that same month, a Minute Book shows that the Queen had read a report from the Jewel Office, and that as a consequence, 'The Queen grants the watermen their old badges'.[19]

Treasury Warrants of 28 June 1708 provide the following detail: 'Subscription by Treasurer Godolphin for the execution of a Lord Chamberlain's warrant dated June 25 to John Charlton, Master of the Jewel House, for 2 new badges each for the Master of the Queen's Barges and the 47 watermen in ordinary: same not to exceed 50 ounces. (Warrant struck through)'[20]

After Queen Anne died in 1714, George I came to the throne. As was customary, new badges were ordered by Lord Chamberlain's warrant to the Master of the Jewel House, 'to deliver to Christopher Hill, Master of His Majesty's Barges, 48 pair of silver badges for the [King's] watermen's liveries not exceeding 50 ounces each and one pair of 60 ounces for himself to an estimate of £1,600.'[21]

Today, the badges, known as 'plastrons', are of silver gilt and made up of a centrepiece depicting the crown supported by a rose and a thistle, with separate letters of 'E' and 'R'.

In 1990, some of the plastrons showed signs of paint, red on the rose and green on the thistle. After consultation with the Palace Comptroller, it was decided to have all the plastrons regilded and to standardise them all into the gold finish. The black shoes of the Royal Watermen were changed at this time to gold-coloured buckle fasteners rather than the lace-up design previously used.

Robert Crouch, who was Bargemaster at this time, also gained permission for Royal Watermen to design a uniform for off-duty use. On one occasion Her Majesty was attended by her Watermen in the West India Dock for a vessel christening without wearing full ceremonial uniform. It was decided that they should wear black blazers with the Royal arms badge, white trousers, a black yachting cap with badges and the Royal Watermen's tie.

Wages

In general, the Royal Bargemaster was paid a fee per annum plus a daily rate, as were his deputy (or the Consort's Bargemaster) and the Royal Watermen. However, early records do not mention a yearly wage. In 1463, Robert Bigger was being paid 7½*d* per day, and records show that in 1516 John Thurston was still being paid that rate.

Wages were generally paid each quarter, with daily rates applied for by the Master of the Barges for himself and the Royal Watermen as and when he saw fit: '6th May 1715 – Christopher Hill, Master of the Barges on £100 per annum, for Lady Day Quarter £25.'[22]

Payment of the Bargemasters' wages was not always as prompt as might have been:

13th April 1668 – John Warner Master of the King's Barges in part of £82 10*s* 0*d* arrear on his fee of £30 per an.[23]

18th April 1677 – £30 Mr J Warner for one year on his fee as Master of His Majesty's barges; in part of 5 years' arrears due thereon to Christmas.

1st February 1703 – two reports of Mr William Vanburgh to the Lord High Treasurer, as to the claims of the Queen's watermen to a year and a half's salary in arrears to them.

Regarding the latter, it was minuted that, 'The year to be paid out of arrears and ye ½ year out of ye Queen's money.' In the same document is a Memorandum 'to move ye Queen that there shall be no more penconary watermen'. Her Majesty was evidently not moved by this, as there were still pensionary Watermen some years later.[24]

There were occasional bonuses paid for 'shooting the bridge'. Passing under Old London Bridge could be a rather dangerous undertaking for a barge, royal or otherwise, and required great skill by the Bargemaster and oarsmen. Old London Bridge had nineteen arches built on 'starlings'. These starlings, together with two water wheels, impeded the flow of the river. When the tide was coming in or going out, the water on each side of the starlings could differ by as much as 6ft, creating a raging torrent underneath the bridge.

Passengers would usually disembark on one side of the bridge, walk across to the other side and then board a barge waiting there to continue their journey. This obviously added extra time to the journey. Those who were in a hurry, or had a taste for excitement, could offer a bonus to their oarsmen to 'shoot the bridge'.

Shooting the bridge could be very dangerous, depending on the prevailing conditions. It was said in those days that the bridge was 'for wise men to pass over, and for fools to pass under'.

There is an account of an attempt to shoot the bridge that went horribly wrong:

On the 8th of November, 1429, the Duke of Norfolk, with many a gentleman, squire, and yeoman, took his barge at St. Mary Overie's between four and five in the evening and purposed to pass through London Bridge, where the aforesaid barge through misgovernment of the man steering, fell upon the piles and was upset; which was the cause of the spilling of many a gentleman and others to their cost. But, by God's help, the Duke and two or three persons seeing the danger leapt upon the piles and so were saved, through the help of them that were above upon the bridge, casting down ropes and so bringing them up safely.[25]

Another description of this, giving the year as 1428, says, 'The vij day of Novembyr the Duke of Northefolke wolde have rowed thorough the brygge of London, and hys barge was rente agayne the arche of the sayde brygge, and there were drowned many men.'[26]

On 6 July 1641, Anne Kirke, one of Queen Henrietta Maria's dressers, was travelling in the Queen's Barge when, whilst shooting the bridge, the barge hit an obstacle (some say a log) and overturned. Everyone in the barge was saved apart from Anne Kirke, who was drowned. It is not known if the Bargemaster and his Watermen were paid their bonus on this occasion!

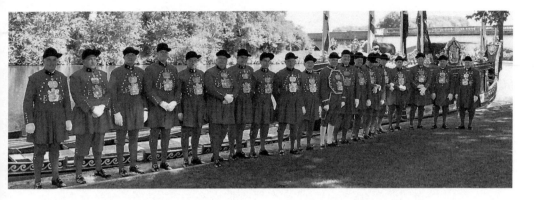

HM Bargemaster Paul Ludwig with a full crew of eighteen Royal Watermen oarsmen at Windsor Home Park. (Personal collection, Paul Ludwig, HM Bargemaster)

Today's Bargemaster and Royal Watermen do not receive any payment. In 1990, it was decided that they could claim for the travel expenses when called for duty. Some decided not to claim these expenses as they felt that the honour of being appointed was payment enough. All uniforms are kept at St James's Palace, where the men muster before each duty. Once changed, they are taken by Palace transport to wherever the duty is taking place. After the event they are usually provided with lunch at either Windsor or Buckingham Palace. On occasion, if time permits, they are encouraged to converse with the public watching the event, giving an opportunity to explain something of their role and history which seems to be much appreciated by the bystanders.

VII

KEEPING IT IN
THE FAMILY

There were several 'dynasties' among the Royal Bargemasters, namely the Warners, the Masons, the Hills and the Robertsons.

The Warners

The Warner family were the most dominant of those families producing more than one Royal Bargemaster.

The first of the Warner Bargemasters was Richard Warner, who was followed by his son, also Richard Warner. Next came Nowell (sometimes Noel), who was succeeded by his son John Warner, followed by his son, another John.

Their 'reign', if one might call it that, lasted for over 100 years from 1604–1713, though from 1648 until his reinstatement in 1662, Nowell Warner did not function as he had been dismissed by Parliament for his Royalist sympathies. However, one could argue that, from a Royalist perspective, Parliament had no authority to dismiss a Royal appointee and that he had remained at his post and was confirmed in his place by Charles II.

The Calendar of State Papers for 1648 records that information had been laid against Nowell Warner and one Mr Arthur. It was alleged that they had been 'great promoters of disaffection' and that they were to be apprehended and any arms in their possession seized.

The Warners were mainly from East Greenwich, and a number of them were buried in the church of St Alphage. Evidence for this comes from both the parish registers and also from *The Environs of London: Counties of Hertfordshire, Essex and Kent* by Daniel Lysons, which relates:

> [T]ombs of the following person, now either removed or become illegible: ... Richard Warner Esq, sometime Master of the Barges to Queen Elizabeth, 1612; Richard Warner jun Esq Master of the Barges to King James 1625; Richard Warner, merchant 1653; Nowell Warner Esq (sone of Richard Warner the younger) Master of the Barges to Charles I and Charles II 1662; John Warner Esq Master of the Barges to Charles II, James II and King William 1694.

When Nowell died in 1662, he was buried by the Great North Door at St Alphage's with his father and grandfather.

This dynasty of Royal Bargemasters were not content just to hold that office, but were businessmen as well. Their business interests included exporting lampreys, owning and running a ferry, as well as property interests.

As far as we know the Warner family's first foray into the contentious world of lampreys, or lamperns as they are sometimes known, began in 1615. By Letters Patent given at Westminster and dated 25 April 1615, James I granted Richard Warner of Greenwich, Master of the King's barges, the sole right to transport lampreys alive from the Thames to Holland and Zealand on payment of 20 marks a year, provided he exported as many as required. Lampreys are a type of jawless fish which resemble eels, and were at that time used to catch ling and cod. Their previous claim to fame was that Henry I is supposed to have died from eating too many of them!

Although Richard Warner had only held the patent since April 1615, by November 1616 there were already problems between him and the Thames fishermen. On 26 November 1616, the Council informed the Treasurer that:

> [O]n consideration of the controversy between the Thames fishermen and the Master of the King's barge, relative to the transportation of lampreys, it is ordered, that, until Christmas 1617, the officers of customs allow the fishermen to transport their lampreys, paying the customs thereon, and 1s per thousand, to Richard Warner, Master of his Majesty's barge.

No further problems seem to have occurred until the reign of Charles I, who had granted a similar licence to Nowell Warner. At Whitehall on

14 March 1636, a report was issued by Thomas, Earl of Arundel and Surrey, and Secretary Windebank, who were referees from His Majesty, of the petition of Nowell Warner, master of his Majesty's barges. The referees ordered that Henry Perkins, Richard Clarke, William Prickett, Robert Benson and William Perkins should give security not to engross any 'lampern' to sell again to any persons that should transport them. It was further ordered that no person, except Nowell Warner by virtue of his licence under the Great Seal, should engross any lamperns, and that no fishermen should take them in the Thames between 20 March and 25 August. Various other regulations were also laid down to prevent the abuses complained of by Warner, and directions given to the Lord Mayor to punish those who had been guilty of throwing gravel and rubbish into the river to further them taking lampreys. On 1 July that year, Nowell Warner petitioned the Council regarding the price of lamperns. The Council referred the petition to the Lord Mayor of London and Sir Henry Marten. This rumbled on for some time.

In 1637, Nowell Warner complained to the Council that the fishermen were trying to force him to take and pay for more lampreys than he could transport, which he said 'would utterly undo him'. On 5 January 1638, there was a full hearing at Whitehall, at the end of which it was ordered by the referees, namely the Lord Privy Seal, the Earl Marshal, the Earl of Dorset and Secretary Windebank, that Warner should thenceforth take from the fishermen 400,000 lampreys at 52s per thousand and no more, unless he required a greater quantity. This should have put an end to the problem, but yet again the fishermen of the Thames petitioned the Council, claiming that Warner had broken the order of 5 January. Subsequently an order was made on 30 May 1638 that, 'finding the fishermen's complaint to be grounded upon no just cause, confirmed the said order, and required the fishermen to forbear to trouble the board any more with such causeless and clamorous petitions'.

Was that the end of the 'Wars of the Lampreys'? No it was not.

The fishermen issued yet another petition on 16 September – this time to the King himself. They accused Warner of having 'of late years endeavoured to undo the petitioners and their families, consisting of above 1,000 persons, by taking their living from them'. It went on, '[Y]our poor supplicants have been forbidden to trouble the Lords any more with their unrelieved oppressions, pray his Majesty to hear their grievances.' They were accusing Warner of having 'by cunning practices' got the whole export trade into his own hands. His Majesty responded by appointing 23 September 1638 to hear their grievances. On that day, their complaints were heard and an Order of the King in Council made. Whist airing their grievances, the fishermen offered to pay the King 20s upon every thousand lampreys exported, or a rent of £600 per annum. It was ordered that the fishermen should attend the Lord Treasurer and Lord Cottingham, who were to treat with them touching their offer. It would appear that the fishermen won the day, as Nowell Warner was required to deliver up the patent. He had not done so by January 1640, as is evidenced by a petition from him saying that before the said patent passed the Great Seal, he made a conveyance to Lyonell Platers and Jerome Laniere of two-thirds of the business and that he had given a bond of 1,000 marks to them that he would not surrender his patent without their consent. Nowell Warner sounds as if he was trying to wriggle out of handing back the patent, but I think his involvement with the lamprey trade was nearing its end.

Richard Warner was allegedly robbed of £15 of gold – quite a sum in the seventeenth century. The Middlesex County Records show that on 20 February 1624 recognisances were taken before Sir Lewes Lewkenor Knt JP, of Richard Askew, victualler, and Francis Salter, silkweaver, both of St Giles-without-Cripplegate, in the sum of £20 each, and Richard Lambert of St Sepulchre's, yeoman, in the sum of £100, for Richard Lambert's appearance 'at the next Sessions to answer the complaint of Richard Warner, Master of the King's Barges, beinge by him suspected to have pickt his pocket, and to have taken away his purse with fifteen pounds of golde in it'.

The involvement of the Warners with owning a ferry began in 1626, when Nowell Warner, then Master of the King's Barge, took out a lease on Potter's Ferry. Although not always known as Potter's Ferry, a ferry between Greenwich and the Isle of Dogs had existed from around the fourteenth century, as it was included when the Manor of Pomfret was sold in 1302. The ferry was certainly part of the Manor of Stepney in the seventeenth century, but possibly it became part of that manor as early as the fifteenth century.

Nowell Warner purchased the lease in 1626 for the annual sum of 20s. Under the lease he was to charge no more than 2d for a man and a horse or 1d for a person alone. The Lord of the Manor's carriages were to be ferried free of charge. It was a repairing lease, so Nowell was obliged to maintain and repair the ferry, including the banks. Samuel Pepys is known to have used the ferry on at least two occasions in 1665, which he describes in his famous diary.

In 1676, Nowell's son, John, purchased the ferry outright. When John Warner, Master of the King's barge, died in 1713, he left to his nephew, John Smith, alias Warner, 'all my ferry at Greenwich with the appurtenances and the piece of ground at or near the landing place on the opposite side of the water'. The family retained the ferry until 1762, when it was sold by Richard Warner for 15 guineas to a group of Greenwich Watermen. This sale gave rise to the Potter's Ferry Society, which continued to operate the ferry. The Warners were wealthy enough to sell some of their houses to the King, but had to wait years to be paid for them! There is a Royal Sign Manual for £75 4s 9d to John Warner, Master of the King's Barge, for the interest from 29 September 1674 to September 1675 on an order No. 781, for £1,254, registered on the Hearth Money, being in compensation for two houses at Greenwich purchased by the King, 'which order would have been paid 31st December 1672 if there had been no restraint of payments in our Exchequer'. A money warrant hereon was dated 2 December. This situation continued for at least another 12 years.

In 1687, a similar Royal Sign Manual for the same amount was for '6% interest for one year to Sept 29 last on £1,254 due to him by an order No. 781 registered on the Hearth Money, being the purchase price of two houses at Greenwich, purchased from him by Charles II'.[1]

The other Royal Bargemaster 'dynasties' include the following:
    The Hills
        Daniel Hill – appointed 1685. Died 24 May 1687 at Lambeth.
        Christopher Hill – elder son of Daniel.
        John Hill – son of Daniel and brother of John.
    The Masons
        Robert Mason – appointed 14 September 1762.
        John Mason – appointed 1736. Died 1768.
        Robert Mason – appointed 1768. Died 1773.
    Roberts
        Richard Roberts – appointed 1796. Resigned 1808 in favour of his nephew
        Thomas Alexander Roberts – appointed 1808. Died 1837
        John Roberts – appointed 1846. Died *c.* 1860.

VIII

BARGEHOUSES

There is a long history of leases from the Archbishop of Canterbury of land on which the Royal bargehouses stood at Lambeth.

In 1652, during the Interregnum, a survey of the King's Bargehouse was undertaken:

> A survey of a certain parcel of Building commonly called or knowne by the name of the King's Barghouse lying and being situate on the Bankside within the parish of St Saviours in ye County of Surrey late parcel of the possessions of Charles Stuart late King of England. All that parcel of buildings as aforesaid built of timber and covered with tyle containing in length Sixty six foote and in breadth Twenty six foote together with all and singular the wasteground to the same belonging. And all stairs passages waters watercourses liberties priviledges profits comodities and advantages to the same any waies belonging or heretofore appertaining.
>
> The foresaid Bargehouse is adjoining and bounded with the wharf or timberyard now in the possession of Griffith Kent towards the west, the river of Thames towards the north and the common causeway or landing place towards the east.
>
> The foresaid Bargehouse is much out of repaires and was the Bargehouse wherein the late King's Barge of State was usually kept which said Barge is now remaining therein and seized on by the trustees for sale of the late King's Goods etc. who intend to dispose of the same to sale and that the Rt Hon Counsell of State have ordered other Bargehouses to be built for their use which are already finished.[1]

In March 1694, a letter to Mr Travers (Surveyor General of Crown Lands) recorded:

> My lords approve your report on the Archbishop of Canterbury's memorial for [my Lords] taking new leases on their Majesties' behalf of certain barge houses etc belonging to him and in the several occupations of their Majesties' barge masters. Your name is to be used as trustee for their Majesties for a lease of same from the Archbishop to the Crown for 21 years at £270 fine and rent of £3 per ann ... The lease is to secure so much land as may be necessary for access to every part of the said barge houses.[2]

The bargehouses were damaged by a storm in 1704. John Warner, the Royal Bargemaster, petitioned the Offices of Work regarding the damage, which in turn submitted a report on the damage.[3]

The following matter pertaining to the bargehouse was recorded on 25 May 1716:

> William Lowndes to Mr Cholmley. I have read to my Lords yours of 15 inst, to wit that which is and always has been called the Princ's Bargehouse, may be taken for the use of his Royal Highness either in your own name or such other as the Prince shall appoint in trust for him, he paying one third of the fine and rent. Please acquaint the Prince's Council with this.
>
> My Lords further desire that you will treat with the said Archbishop in relation to the fine to be paid for the said three Bargehouses in order to the apportioning the rent and fine and to take a lease in your own name to the said Bargehouses and Bargemaster's house in trust for his Majesty, who is to bear the other two thirds of the fine and rent. Please report to my Lords the terms of yr agreement with the Archbishop so that they may direct the issue of the money to discharge the King's part of the fine.

This was followed on 6 June the same year by the following:

> Money warrant for £225 3s 6d to Hugh Cholmley, Esq, Surveyor General of Crown Lands: without account: to be by him applied and paid over to satisfy to the Archbishop of Canterbury the £180 fine of a lease [made by the said Archbishop] to the said Cholmley for the use of the Crown of two Bargehouses at or near Lambeth, Co. Surrey, with a dwelling house

and other appurtenances thereto and also to satisfy the fees and charges (being in all £45 3s 6d) on executing the said lease. (Money order dated June 8 hereon).[4]

In February 1729, Robert Mason complained that the bargehouses were so ruinous that the State Barges would be spoiled by the weather if they were not speedily repaired. His representations were acted upon, and a Report of the Board of Works dated 15 April the same year estimated that repairs would cost £150. On 21 May, a warrant was issued from the Lords of the Treasury for the Board of Works 'to undertake repairs in connection with the barge houses commanded by His Majesty, so the charge do not exceed the estimated £150'.

The lease of the two bargehouses and the Bargemaster's house at Lambeth, held by the Archbishop of Canterbury, was renewed on 1 February 1733.[5]

The Bargehouse and the Bargemaster's house at Lambeth were the subject of a renewal of their lease from the Archbishop of Canterbury in 1762:

Mr Martin having transmitted to me the Lord Chamberlains letter signifying his Majesty's pleasure for renewing the lease of his Majesty's Bargehouses and Barge Masters house at Lambeth held of his Grace the Archbishop of Canterbury, Together with your Lordship's directions that I should treat with his Grace and inform your Lordships of the demands made for such renewal, I sent to his Grace accordingly, and am informed by Thomas Parry Esqr his Grace's Secretary who has the care of the affairs relating to his revenue, That a new lease of the premises will be prepared forthwith to pass under his Grace's seal in my name, for his Majesty's use, for a term of Twenty one years from Lady day next 1762, on surrender of the present lease in which there will then be thirteen years unexpired, for a fine of Thirty Pounds Reserving the old rent of Forty Shillings per Ann Which terms I am of opinion are reasonable and may be accepted if your Lordships shall think fit.

The necessary charges attending the premises will be as follows Viz

The fine to the Archbishop	£30-00-00
Fees to his Grace's Secretary	£7-00-00
Reference and Warrant at the Treasury	£2-5-00
To the Receivr of the Land revenue 12p [per] £ on £51	£2-11-00

To the Audr of the Land revenue 3p [per] £ on £51   £ -12-9

Entering the Treasury Warrt with the Auditor   £ -13-4

Soliciting and enrolling the Lease   £8-8-

    I take this opportunity to acquaint your Lordships That the Lease of some ground joing to the Tarras Wall of Windsor Castle held of the Dean and Cannons of Windsor is in Course also to be renewed. And there are some arrears of Rent due to the Dean and Canons, and to the Corporation of New Windsor for ground there held by the Crown, And also some arrears of Land Tax, claimed by the Commissioners of the Land tax concerning which your Lordships will give such directions as you think fit.

    All of which humbly submitted. To your Lordships wisdom.

    K Herbert Suns Genl.

    Feb 2d 176[6]

The King's Bargehouse at Lambeth was certainly still in use in 1808, as letters of resignation from Richard Roberts and Thomas Alexander Roberts gave 'The King's Bargehouse, Lambeth' as their address.

IX

ROYAL BARGES

Since medieval times, the monarch has always had a fleet of barges, vessels of different sizes and types. These ranged from barges used for carrying goods, some of which were sea-going, to the State Barge itself and the shallops and ballingers used by the monarch and his/her family for general travel.

With regards to general travel, it was eventually found that the shallop with eight oarsmen was the best all-round design for Thames use, giving a balance of speed and manoeuvrability. Even today, the Queen has a retinue of Bargemaster and eight Watermen in attendance when on the river, which reflects this historic arrangement.

It should be noted at the outset that it was not just the monarch who had a barge: the consort and other members of the Royal Family had them too, such was the importance of the barge as a means of transport. The barges often had coverings or tilts in the livery colours of their owners.

A royal warrant of Henry VII dated 3 December 1498 'for the King's Barge and Ballinger' gives details of payments made to one Thomas Gwyneth as follows:

Item: for 50 yards of white woollen cloth to cover one side of the king's Barge, price per yard 2s 10d – total £7 20d.
Item: 50 yards of green woollen cloth to cover the other side of the Barge, price per yard 3s 2d [presumably this was more expensive due to the cost of dying the cloth green].
Item: eighteen yards of white woollen cloth to cover one half of the Ballinger, price per yard 2s 10d.

HM Bargemaster William East piloting the Royal Barge through Henley Bridge.

Item: eighteen yards of green woollen cloth to cover the other half of the Ballinger, price per yard 3s 2d.

In *The Great Wardrobe Accounts of Henry VII and Henry VIII* (edited by Maria Hayward), the measurements of the cloth required give us an idea of the size of the barge relative to the size of the Ballinger.

In 1529, Henry VIII also ordered green and white cloth to make tilts for 'our new barge' and 'our little barge'. The payments were to be made to John Johnson, the Royal Bargemaster, rather than the supplier of the cloth.

The Privy Purse Expenses of Elizabeth of York (consort of Henry VII) by Sir Nicholas Harris Nicolas record, in 1502, payment to her Bargemaster Lewes Waltier for 'tallowing, dressing and for roopes and other necessaries for the Quene's barge'. Later that year, William Fowler was paid 'to dying cc xxij yerdes of wardemole blewe and murray for the Quene's barge'.

Henry VIII had a 'great Barge' called *The Lyon* and another called *Greyhound*. In 1532, Anne Boleyn appropriated Queen Katherine's barge and defaced her coat of arms.[1]

In May 1540, John Johnson, master of the King's Barge, was paid 10s 'for his charges in trimming, burning, and tallowing of the King's great barge, called *The Lyon*'. Tallow was used to lubricate the oar leathers in their rowlocks, which also reduced the thumping noise caused by rowing. It is surprising how annoying the sound of 'dry leathers' can be during a long pull. This has been shown up with the revival of Thames traditional rowing or fixed-seat rowing. Tallow has to be carried aboard in a small pot to alleviate this problem.

During the reign of Philip and Mary, a new Royal Barge, emblazoned in silver and gold and with elaborate wainscoting, was commissioned and trimmed with the King and Queen's regalia.[2]

In 1558, the Queen's shipwright, Wylliam Stephin, was paid £20 for making her a new barge called *Leader*.

Sometimes the superstructure of the royal barges would be adapted for specific events. In 1606, the King of Denmark visited London. James I went, with a fleet of barges, to meet him. The superstructure of the King's Barge was altered to look like a floating castle, with battlements attached to the roof. Instead of being rowed, it was towed by another barge that was rowed by thirty Watermen.

In 1593, Paul Hentzner, a German traveller, after visiting the playhouses at Bankside, stated, 'Not far from one of these theatres, which are built of wood, lies the Royal barge, close to the river; it has two splendid cabins, beautifully ornamented with glass windows, painting and gilding, it is kept upon dry ground, and sheltered from the weather.' The Royal Bargehouse would therefore appear to have been at this time at Bankside, by Paris Garden Stairs.[3]

The only surviving pieces of Tudor Royal Barges are two paintings on wood, framed by columns, which were probably part of the decoration of the cabin of Queen Elizabeth's State Barge. The barge had fallen into disuse and was broken up in 1618. Fortunately the paintings were purchased with 'all ye upper part of Queen Elizabeth's State Barge' by Edward Alleyn, the Founder of Dulwich College. He paid £2 2s 6d for them. The paintings are of *Pietas* and *Liberalitas*, and are still carefully preserved at Dulwich College.[4]

In 1610, the household of Prince Henry included his Master of the Barge, William Goring, who received £20 per annum, together with eighteen Watermen in Ordinary.

In 1611, Clement Chapman, his Majesty's joiner, was paid 'the sum of £86 9s 6d, for works by him done about his Majesty's, the Queen's, the Prince's, the Duke of York's, and the Lady Elizabeth's barges'.[5]

The Royal Barges had always been spectacularly ornamented with carvings, and gilded and painted as befitted the status of the monarch.

Two painted panels with columns believed to be from the State Barge of
Elizabeth I, now kept at Dulwich College. (Dulwich Picture Gallery, London)

Horace Walpole, in his *Anecdotes of Painting in England*, mentions John de
Critz (possibly the Elder), Serjeant Painter to the King. Various grants were
made to John de Critz by the King, one being a grant for life jointly with
Leonard Fryer dated 11 May 1605, of the position of Serjeant Painter. The
post encompassed any kind of painting that might be desired, including
work on palaces, carriages and barges.[6]

Walpole cites a memorandum (no date given) that de Critz wrote in his
own hand, describing work he had carried out to the Royal Barge:

John de Critz demandeth allowance for these parcells of Worke following,
viz For repayreing, refreshing, washing and varnishing the whole body of

his Majesty's privy barge, and mending with fine gould and faire colours many and diverse parts thereof, as about the chaire of state, the doors, and most of the antiques about the windows, that had been galled and defaced, the two figures at the entrance being most new coloured and painted, the Mercury and the lion that are fixed to the sternes of this and the row barge being in several places repayred both with gould and colours, as also the tassarils/taffarils on the top of the barge in many parts guilded and strowed with faire byse. The two figures of Justice and Fortitude, most an end [*sic*] being quite new painted and guilded. The border on the outside of the bulk being new layd with faire white and trayled over with greene according to the custom heretofore – and for baying and colouring the whole number of the oares for the row barge being thirty six.

In 1620, an advance payment of £200 was made to Artificers towards the making of a Royal Barge for his Majesty:

to JOHN DE CRITES, his Majesty's serjeant painter, CLEMENT CHAPMAN, joiner, MAXIMILIAN COLT, carver, and WILLIAM BOURDMAN, his Majesty's locksmith, the sum of £200., in part of £400., to be taken to them by way of imprest towards the charge of making a privy barge for his Majesty's service this next Parliament.[7]

The English Civil War took its toll on the Royal Barges. On 15 April 1648, the following order was made by Parliament: 'Ordered, That The Commanders in Chief of the Forces at Whitehall shall have the Use of the King's great tow Barge, the Archbishop's Barge and the Four Oar Barge, for the present Service of the State, and Safety of these Parts.'[8]

Apparently the commanders did not take much care of them, as in 1660, when Charles II had been invited to return to England and reclaim the throne, it would seem there was no longer a Royal Barge in operation.

On 15 May 1660, Nowell Warner, along with the Royal Watermen, submitted a petition which said, 'the Barge called the *Brigantine* was carried away, by what order they knew not. They desire that they have her for His Majesty's service as there is not a barge on the river fit for the purpose but the Earl of Northumberland's.'

A report was made by the Earl of Pembroke from the Committee of Petitions 'that upon the Petition of Warner, Bargeman to His Majesty, he and the other the King's Watermen be forthwith authorised to take into their Care the Barge called *The Brigantine*, there being no other Barge fit for His Majesty's service, and that built with the Public Revenue.'[9]

In 1698, a new Royal Shallop was built for the Queen. The shallop is now in the collection of the National Maritime Museum in Greenwich. The shallop's last voyage was as part of the Peace Pageant which took place on 4 August 1919. This water pageant was held to celebrate the contribution that mariners and merchant seamen made to the war effort. The procession went from London Bridge to Chelsea, and was watched by huge crowds lining the banks of the Thames.

In 1715, a warrant was made for delivery to the Master of the King's Barges of three bear hides, a Turkey work carpet for the bottom of the twelve-oar barge and a velvet carpet trimmed with a narrow gold fringe for the table, and to take out the letter 'A' and put in the letter 'G' in the corner of the tilt. Obviously the changes made to remove the letter 'A' and replace it with the letter 'G' was to reflect the change of monarch at this time, as Queen Anne had died in 1714 and George I had ascended the throne. A new standard to be flown on the Royal Barge was also ordered during that year:

Royal Bargemaster and Watermen conveying HM The Queen to the opening of the River and Rowing Museum at Henley. (Picture by Sue Milton, photographer)

'for the delivery to Mr Christopher Hill, Master of His Majesty's Barges, of a Standard for His Majesty's State Barge, with crimson silk line and a serge bag to put it in.'[10]

In 1717, the Civil List Accounts show that £597 16*s* 4*d* was paid to 'John Loftus, the King's barge-builder, for mending the shallope, six oar barge and their oars, for building etc a new eight oar barge for the King and for gilding etc.the shallope, the twelve oar and six oar barges'.[11]

That same year, further expenditure was approved for crimson Genoa velvet and damask for the new eight-oared Royal Barge.

In 1731, a new barge was built for Frederick, Prince of Wales. The barge was designed by William Kent and constructed at the yard of John Hall. It has beautifully carved woodwork, which was sumptuously gilded in 24ct gold.

Its first task was to take the Prince of Wales, his mother and his sisters from Chelsea Hospital to Somerset House. Two other barges were in attendance, one of which was carrying musicians, with court officials in the other. This barge was used regularly until 1849.[12]

State Barges by Peter Norton

Prince Frederick's barge was last used by the Royal Family on 30 October 1849, when it carried Prince Albert and Prince Edward (later Edward VII) from Whitehall Stairs to the City, where the Prince Consort opened the new Coal Exchange. Prince Frederick's barge is now on exhibition at the National Maritime Museum at Greenwich.

In 1755, whilst Prince Frederick's barge was still in use, the Prince of Wales (later George III) had a new leisure barge built to mark his birthday. It was a ten-seat barge, but it is not known how many of the seats were for the oarsmen. The barge was named *The Princess Augusta* and is described thus: 'It is finished in a taste entirely new, and made to imitate a swan swimming; the imitation is so very natural, as hardly to be distinguished from a real bird, except from its size; the neck and head rise to the height of eighteen feet, the body forms a commodious cabin.'[13]

All we have of earlier Royal Barges are two panels from the interior of one of Elizabeth I's barges, now in the possession of Dulwich College.

In 1884–85, a new barge was built for and given to Queen Victoria by the Admiralty. According to Mr Nutt, the resident architect at Windsor Castle, the last occasion that the King's State Barge was used was 13 June 1904 when the King and Queen were rowed by the King's Watermen, under the charge of Mr East, from the Home Park to Eton College to receive an address. It was kept at Virginia Water until 1936, when it was given to the Commander-in-Chief, Portsmouth.

Below is a transcript of a letter regarding this barge sent to the Secretary of the Admiralty by the Director of the National Maritime Museum on 25 April 1958:

I placed your letter of the 7th February, reference M.111/34/56, before my Trustees at their meeting on the 10th April.

1. There was a full attendance on this day, HRH The Duke of Edinburgh being among the Trustees present, and the kind offer of Their Lordships to make the Royal Barge, presented to HM Queen Victoria by the Lords Commissioners on the occasions of her Jubilee, available for the National Maritime Museum, in accordance with the suggestion made by HM King Edward VIII in 1936, was duly considered.

2. While my Trustees greatly appreciated this offer, and I was instructed to request you that you would please be good enough to convey their thanks to My Lords Commissioners of the Admiralty, they were also mindful of the fact that we already have in this Museum preserved and on exhibition in a special Barge House built for the purpose, two Royal State Barges, namely, the Queen's Shallop of 1689, and the barge of Frederick, Prince of Wales, of 1732, also two of the Commissioners' barges from Chatham.

3. In these circumstances, the addition of a further example, beautiful though it is, of this type of craft, could only be regarded as a luxury, which it would be selfish to accept.

4. My Trustees were unanimously and strongly of the opinion that if this craft, built as a State Barge for Queen Victoria, were offered to the Maritime Museum of Canada at Halifax, NS it would be received with warm gratitude and very great enthusiasm by the Canadian Authorities.

5. The Chairman of the Maritime Museum at Halifax, which is being developed into the Canadian equivalent of the National Maritime Museum at Greenwich, is Rear-Admiral H. F. Pullen, OBECD, Flag Officer Atlantic Coast. There is thus a very close link between this Museum and the Royal Canadian Navy; and it is also not without significance that this year commemorates the 200th anniversary of the opening of the Dockyard at Halifax.

6. I was therefore directed, in replying to your letter, to suggest that My Lords Commissioners of the Admiralty might ask HM The Queen whether she would be graciously pleased to offer this Royal Barge to the Maritime Museum of Canada.

7. In the event of Her Majesty approving of this proposal, I am informed by one of my Trustees, who is Director of a Shipping Company, that the Cunard Line would be only too pleased to arrange for the transportation of the Barge to Halifax, if so requested, without making any charge of any kind. If, therefore, my Trustees' suggestion is favoured, the matter proceeds further, and it is desired to accept the offer of the Cunard Line, would you please get in touch direct with the Managing Director, Frank Dawson, Esq, CBE, Cunard Steamship Co. Ltd., Cunard Building, Liverpool 3, who will be only too pleased to take whatever steps are necessary.

8. I understand from Mr. Dawson that the Cunard Line have a very deep interest in the Maritime Museum at Halifax, and have helped the Museum already in very many ways. This makes it particularly pleasant for them to offer to transport the Royal Barge if the matter should arise.

9. I am also enclosing herewith a copy of an old photograph of the Royal Barge when it was in Tims' Boathouse at Staines for repair rather over 50 years ago. I have a considerable amount of information concerning the history of the Barge, partly from Messrs. Tims, the Boatbuilders, and also largely culled from the records of the Lord Chamberlain's Office at St. James's Palace. No doubt the Admiralty records contain many details, if there is any further information which I can supply, I shall be happy to do so.

10. I understand that the Barge was built in 1884/5 by Burgoynes, Hampton Wick, Kingston; and that the dimensions are 34ft. x 6ft. 3in. She was kept at Virginia Water until 1936, when she was transferred to the Commander-in-Chief, Portsmouth.

11. I am, Sir, Your obedient Servant, Frank G. G. Carr Director.[14]

An undated article describes this barge as having a teak interior, painted white, with gold scrollwork. Green silk hangings were a feature of the interior, with gold mouldings and carvings. The stern featured the Royal Arms beautifully carved in mahogany. Over the state room was a green silk canopy supported by six fluted columns with ornamental bases. Large brass dolphins were mounted on the gunwales of the barge, their tails forming rowlocks.

The figurehead was also a dolphin, carved in mahogany and etched with gold. A serpent tiller was fixed to the rudder.

Royal Barges used since Queen Elizabeth II came to the throne in 1952 have often been hired for the occasion and given the temporary title of Royal Barge. MV *Havengore* is a case in point. This vessel, owned by the Port of London Authority, was used on many occasions for special river events, the funeral river progress of Sir Winston Churchill being the most memorable. *Havengore* is a Nelson 61 vessel, built by Tough Brothers, in 1955, with GRP hull and wooden superstructure. During the 1970s, another PLA vessel, MV *Nore*, began to be used; *Royal Nore*, as it is now known, is the prestige royal and diplomatic launch for London. In late 2006, Gillingham Marina redesigned the vessel and undertook a 'life extension programme' for the owners, the Port of London Authority. It was eventually named as the official Royal Barge and was permanently crewed by a Royal Waterman. During its many years of service, it became synonymous with all Royal events on the tidal part of the river, through even into modern times.

In the 1980s, a replica Royal Barge shallop was built and given to the Watermen's Company for safekeeping. It was named *Jubilant* to honour the

MV *Havengore*, sometimes used as the Royal Barge on the tidal Lower Thames. (Picture by Sue Milton, photographer)

MV *Royal Nore* in Greenwich Reach, with the Bargemaster and eight Watermen attending Her Majesty the Queen. (Personal collection of R.G. Crouch)

Queen's Silver Jubilee. However, being oar-powered, it never replaced *Nore* as the official Royal Barge. Two other shallops were built during these years: *Royal Thamesis*, an upper Thames vessel, which in spite of its grand name, is and was not an official Royal Barge; and the shallop barge *Jubilant*, stationed on the tidal Thames below Teddington. Both vessels, being oar-powered, were only used as support vessels in river pageants, not as official Royal Barges.

Nore has been the official Royal Barge throughout most of Her Majesty's reign, and has earnt its place in Thames history. *Nore* was built by Camper & Nicholsons in Gosport and launched in March 1951. It was commissioned by the Port of London Authority as one of their harbourmaster's launches, with additional use as Her Majesty's Royal Barge. It was operated by the PLA for more than twenty years in this role. The 14-ton MV *Nore* is powered by twin diesel engines, giving a maximum speed of approximately 20 knots.

In 1953, *Nore* was adapted for use during the coronation programme of HM Queen Elizabeth II and was designated the 'Royal Barge'. The vessel transported the Queen and Prince Philip on 12 June 1953 from a banquet at the Guildhall to the Royal Festival Pier.

Nore has had a memorable Thames career, carrying members of British and European royal families. It has also carried many foreign Heads of State, including US President Truman, Khrushchev of the USSR, General de Gaulle of France and many Commonwealth Prime Ministers. It also led Sir Winston Churchill's Thames funeral procession in 1965.

It was decommissioned in the early 1970s and renamed *King's Reach*, passing to a scout troop, who then sold it on to Middle Eastern owners.

It was rediscovered by the present owners in an Essex boatyard. They purchased and restored it at an estimated cost of £100,000. It was moved to Mitchell's Boatyard in Poole harbour, where it was prepared for a full refit. With rebuilt engines, it was re-registered under its original name in London.

The NORE Restoration Project Ltd has now been established and, when the work is complete, it will once again take its place as a prominent feature of the River Thames. *Nore* will be crewed by Freemen of the River Thames and by Her Majesty's Watermen. As well as its royal duties, it will be used for educational projects and will also be available for private and corporate charter, offering clients a unique insight into Britain's and the Thames' ceremonial heritage.

Gloriana: A Row-Barge for the Queen

Royal Barges as a method of travel for the monarch have in the past needed to be fast and manoeuvrable, and today the motorised vessels *Nore* and *Windrush*, which are used as Her Majesty's Barges on the Tideway and up-river, both fill this role of speed and ease of use very well. However, the other role of a Royal Barge is ceremonial, and with the increase in numbers of people wishing to attend river events, a requirement for high carrying capacity is an added consideration.

Oared vessels on the Thames of today have a big disadvantage due to the much-changed tidal regime. The encroachment of the riverbanks and the embanking of the Thames have caused a faster and stronger tide flow, making rowing against the tide almost impossible over any meaningful distance. An oar-powered vessel is therefore out of the question for transport purposes. Several attempts at building an eight-oared fast shallop have been

Lord Jeffrey Sterling, Baron Sterling of Plaistow. (Picture by permission of the Gloriana Trust)

attempted, but although these vessels are beautiful and well-built, they are not practical when compared with a motorised vessel. However, the building of these 55ft shallops did prove that the old boatbuilding skills still exist on the Thames of today.

The idea for a waterborne tribute to the Queen for her Diamond Jubilee came from Charles, Prince of Wales, and along with the planning of the great river parade, Lord Sterling proposed the building of a full-sized State Barge, a row-barge for the Queen to be named *Gloriana*, to be used in the Jubilee celebrations. The idea caught on, and Lord Sterling took on the financing of the project personally. The construction cost of the row-barge was estimated at £1.5m, with additional financial donations being received from Mr Eyal Ofer, The Gosling Foundation, The Weston Foundation, Lloyds Register and The Stiftelsen Kristian Gerhard Jebsen Foundation.

The Gloriana Trust was formed and, with the support of the Maritime Heritage Trust and their chairman David Morgan, the early stages of design and construction were initiated. It would be a motivation for national pride, a showcase for traditional British boatbuilding and craftsmanship and a means of encouraging people to engage with the River Thames and the sport of rowing.

Design and construction

Gloriana is designed as a 90ft-long (27m) eighteen-oared rowing barge, with oarsmen sitting two abreast in nine pairs. To help cope with today's tide strength, it is also powered by two electric inboard engines. It can carry an additional thirty-four persons, including crew. The design was inspired by Canaletto's London paintings of eighteenth-century livery barges, resembling the style of vessel used by Lord Mayors for their showing to the City in a parade which originally took place on the river.

A labour of love

Construction began in November 2011 at Brentford. A team of two naval architects, Stuart Roy and Ed Burnett, worked with the Project Manager, Damian Byrne MVO, the build team being led by master boatbuilder Mark Edwards of Richmond Bridge Boathouses, who has built shallops and several Watermen cutters for various City livery companies who support the fixed-seat code of traditional rowing.

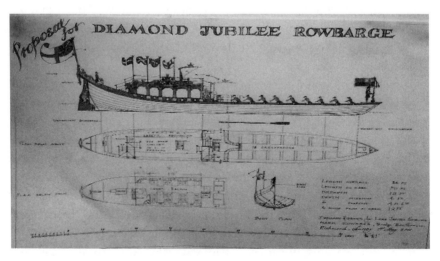

(Personal collection of R.G. Crouch)

(Pictures by Malcolm Knight, Gloriana Trust)

Gloriana is built of wood using traditional methods; this includes sweet chestnut flooring sourced from trees from Prince Charles's estate. The ornate carvings were made by Polygon Scenery and finished in gold leaf with fine hand painting by Hare & Humphreys. Its ornately decorated oars were made by J. Sutton Blades, oar-makers since the 1970s.

On 19 April 2012, *Gloriana* was transported by road from the workshop to the River Thames and launched into the water at Isleworth.

The Queen officially named *Gloriana* on 25 April 2012, as a legacy to mark her Diamond Jubilee. Her Majesty has asked that the vessel be retained by Lord Sterling and the new charitable trust to be used to promote better use of the Thames. It will provide opportunities for charities, to take part in celebrations on the Thames, particularly in events for the young.

The Diamond Jubilee Pageant

Gloriana was the lead vessel in the Thames Diamond Jubilee Pageant, a parade of over 1,000 boats. Among the eighteen rowers were Olympic gold medallists Sir Steve Redgrave and Sir Matthew Pinsent, Jonny Searle, Guin Batten, Miriam Batten and Ben Hunt-Davis, as well as British servicemen Will Dixon, Rory Mackenzie and Neil Heritage, who lost limbs in Iraq and Afghanistan. The crew wore a uniform of royal blue tracksuits, T-shirts and caps.

After the Diamond Jubilee, this new State Barge has settled into its role as an echo of the Thames's history. Its fine build quality and striking looks are a reminder of the royal use of the river. *Gloriana* continues to be involved with many of the Thames river events.

In May 2012, fine weather welcomed the vessel at Hampton Court Palace as it prepared to leave for the annual Royal Watermen's marathon row to deliver the River Water Stela to The Tower of London. It was escorted by several City Livery company in their cutters, dressed overall for the occasion. Named the Tudor Pull, it is an ongoing tribute to honour the traditions and heritage of England and the River Thames.

X

PALACES AND LANDING PLACES

Before watergates and river stairs were commonplace, vessels like shallops and wherries would have to land bow-into the shore, often meaning a muddy landing for passengers. Stairs would be built into the wall of a building, but at low tide it still meant a walk up the beach. This problem was overcome by the building of a causeway made of timber planking. This could become very slippery, and Watermen were expected to carry sand to spread onto the greasy planks for the better grip of footwear.

To overcome a vessel's bow sticking into the mud, crushed chalk would be placed alongside the causeway. Some vessels, like wherries, were adapted

View of Chelsea Watergate in the seventeenth century.

with slightly curved keels, this clever design allowing a Waterman to bring his boat gently alongside with its bow just touching the chalk. As the passengers moved forward to disembark, their weight pushed the keel into the chalk and made the boat feel solid and safe. When new passengers embarked the opposite happened; as they walked aft to take their seats, the bow would rise and float clear of the chalk, thus allowing the Waterman to disembark and embark his passengers without leaving his rowing bench.

The wealthy would have stone stairs built as a river entrance to their property. The tide difference centuries ago was just a few feet, but as the river was embanked, particularly in Victorian times, the tidal range became greater, making it necessary to develop floating piers with bridges to connect to the shore.

The importance and usage of the Royal palaces along the Thames changed over the centuries. As England, rather than France, and London, rather than Winchester, became the monarchy's base, so the emphasis on travel by the Thames increased in importance. More palaces along the banks of the Thames were built and movement between them increased.

Westminster

The Palace of Westminster was the principle residence of the Royal Family from the eleventh century until it was destroyed by fire in 1512.

In medieval times, according to plans of the palace, there were two bridges – the King's Bridge by the Water Gate and the Queen's Bridge to the west of the complex.

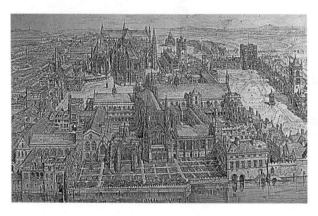

View of the medieval Palace of Westminster, showing the river access point of the Black Rod Stairs, which are sadly rarely used.

River view showing the old Traitor's Gate river entrance.

Tower of London

The Tower was the first of the Norman strongholds to be built by the Thames. The oldest part of the Tower complex, the White Tower, was begun on the orders of William the Conqueror in the 1070s and completed by 1100. Built as a fortress, it later became a royal residence.

Henry III built a watergate, St Thomas's Tower, in 1230, to give him direct access to the Tower from the Thames. Edward I built the watergate which forms part of St Thomas's Tower. Edward III built another watergate for his private use below the Cradle Tower.

Under the Tudors, the Tower was used less and less as a royal residence, but continued to play a significant part in the first stage of the coronations until James I.

Windsor

The early part of the castle was built by William the Conqueror and it is still used regularly by Queen Elizabeth II.

Windsor Castle. (Library of Congress)

York Place

York Place was built close to Westminster *c.*1240 by the Archbishop of York, and was much enlarged by Cardinal Wolsey until it rivalled if not surpassed the royal residences. Henry VIII acquired it in 1528 prior to the downfall of Wolsey in 1530.

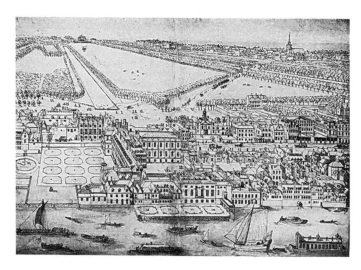

York Place.

Whitehall

There were always two landing places at Whitehall – a public one and the Privy Stairs. The Privy Stairs were situated beyond the Chapel, on what would later become the grounds of 6 Whitehall Place.

According to Simon Thurley's *The Vanishing Architecture of the River Thames*, Henry VIII commissioned a new private bridge in 1530, which was the most impressive of all the royal landing stages. It was supported on stone cutwaters, and the timber-framed structure had two storeys and a terrace on its roof. Stairs led up from the river to a gallery, which led to Henry's own lodgings. Whitehall was where the royal barge was usually kept. The Bargemaster and the Royal Watermen had offices and storerooms nearby.

In 1529/30, a payment was made to Nedam, the King's carpenter, for work carried out to the Privy Stairs. The Privy Stairs were only to be used by the monarch, the Royal Family and certain members of the Court:

> Whereas greate noise and disorders are made at the privy Staires by all sortes of Watermen comeing there and plying, and landing fares and persons there, whereby His Majesty is disturbed goeing into His Barge, I doe therefore hereby Order That noe Watermen Whatsoever But the King's and Queen's Watermen doe presume to ply any fares there, or bring theire

Whitehall. (Image by Whitemay)

Boates there or land any persons there at theire perrills. Except only if any Gentleman belonging to ye Court ... The Great Gate being Shutt may be there landed, but ye Watermen to depart thence and not to stay there or receave any fare at these staires at theire perrills.

However, by 1691 the old Tudor stairs were deemed inadequate and a new terrace was ordered to be built. At 285ft long and 70ft deep, with elegant curving steps and a central privy landing stage, it was designed to be an elegant backdrop for the kind of ceremonial occasions then in favour with the monarchy. Even after Whitehall was destroyed by fire and St James's Palace became the monarchy's principal seat, the landing stage remained in use.[1]

Richmond

Richmond Palace began life as Shene Palace. Shene Palace was rebuilt by Henry VII *c.*1501 and he renamed it Richmond Palace. It was the favourite home of Elizabeth I, and during her reign she had a new landing place built in 1584–85. It is thought to have had a broad landing stage, with a narrower jetty extending into the river.[2]

Richmond Palace, demolished in the years after the death of King Charles I.

Baynard's Castle

On the edge of the Thames by the Fleet River, Baynard's Castle was the London base of the House of York during the Wars of the Roses. The Norman structure was demolished in 1213. Rebuilt by Henry VII and acting as his main residence, it was later given to Katherine of Aragon by Henry VIII. It survived until 1666, when it was burned down in the Great

Fire of London. A drawing of it is kept at the British Museum, showing a stone bridge with two arches leading to stairs down to the Thames.

Baynard's Castle from the river, showing the landing causeway.

Bridewell

This was Henry VIII's main London residence for the first part of his reign. It had river access via a watergate and river stairs.

Hampton Court

Thomas Wolsey took a lease on the property in 1514 and proceeded to build a vast complex until he relinquished it to Henry VIII in 1528.

At this time the River Thames was tidal at least as far as Hampton Court. When rowing to the Tower or Greenwich, it had to be remembered that there was a variation in the water level at London Bridge ranging from 15ft to over 20ft. Henry VIII had a clock installed at Hampton Court which gave the times of high and low tides at London Bridge.

Henry also began to build a more impressive riverside entrance, which is described by Simon Thurley thus:

> In 1536, the King began the construction of a structure known as the Water Gallery at the south end of his gardens next to the river. This remarkable building was part landing stage, part barge house and part pleasure pavilion. It allowed the royal barge to moor under cover and Henry to disembark in privacy and comfort.

Row-Barge *Gloriana* at Hampton Court Palace Landing. (Picture by Sue Milton, photographer)

Greenwich

Built by Humphrey Duke of Gloucester in 1443, Greenwich became a royal residence when Margaret of Anjou acquired it after the arrest and death of the duke in 1447. Henry VII rebuilt it between 1498 and 1504.

Henry VIII, Mary I and Elizabeth I were all born there. Greenwich became the most important Tudor palace after the royal apartments were destroyed by

fire in 1512. It fell into disrepair during the Civil War, and while Charles II intended to rebuild it, the works were never completed.

Greenwich Palace showing the Watergate, with a shallop barge and a wherry in the foreground.

Kew

KEW PALACE.

Kew was remodelled by Frederick, Prince of Wales, when he leased the White House *c.* 1730, which was close to the Dutch House where his sisters lived.

View of Kew Palace looking down-river towards the City. (Image by Duncan, 1890)

Somerset House

Originally built by the Duke of Somerset, uncle to Edward VI, in the 1540s, when Somerset was executed in 1532 the property passed to the Crown. It was finished in 1553 and was home to Princess Elizabeth until she became Queen in 1558.

The bargehouse entrance to Somerset House. The top part of the arch can still be seen today, but is now obscured by the Embankment.

As road transport became more practical, great palaces and houses along the
Thames moved their entrances away from the river to access the roadway system.

Later it became the home of James I's queen, Anne of Denmark, and
became known as Denmark House. In 1609, work began to transform
Denmark House, which included a privy entrance from the Thames called
the 'Quenes staires'. A 190ft covered walkway led from the river to the
Queen's gallery, from which stairs led to her private apartments.[3]

Somerset House later became the home of Queen Henrietta Maria. After
the restoration, Henrietta Maria returned to Denmark House. Catherine of
Braganza, wife of Charles II, lived there from 1685 until 1693, and was the
last Queen to live there.

The Future

It has been said that the ancient appointments of a Royal Bargemaster
and Watermen are outdated and have become outmoded. However, many
would argue that they still have an important role to play in the twenty-first
century, providing a reference to the past from which we can learn, giving a
timeline leading into the present era which supports the unique system by
which we administrate our country.

Her Majesty bidding farewell after her family trip aboard the State Row-Barge *Gloriana* at Windsor Home Park in 2016. (Picture by Malcolm Knight, Gloriana Trust)

Her Majesty's Bargemasters and Watermen feel honoured to play their part within England's traditions; they trust that they are creating a legacy for future rivermen to support the richness and colour of our British system. It is comforting to think that, after over 800 years, during which time so many changes have taken place on the Thames, the ancient convention of appointing Watermen to the Royal Household is still taking place, involving them with the pageantry of Royal events.

It is indeed reassuring to know that like the Company of Watermen's long-established apprenticeship system, which even with modern navigation requirements and new forms of boat propulsion, is still found to be the best method for training and teaching young people the skills of river work, the appointment of Watermen to the monarch still has relevance within our modern world and has an important role to play in the future.

Her Majesty's Bargemasters

The honour of becoming HM Bargemaster is still a very sought-after appointment among the river fraternity. Like many of England's traditions developed over time, it might seem at first glance to be inconsequential and

The new Royal Bargemaster on his first Royal duty with Lord Vesty, who was on his last duty as Master of Horse, flanked by Royal Watermen. From left to right, R. Coleman, D. Ludwig, J. McCarthy, C Livett, Lord Vesty, S. McCarthy, P. Prentice, D. Arnold and T. Keetch. (Picture by kind permission of S. McCarthy, HM Waterman)

outdated, but on closer examination the merit of this institution becomes more evident. Men from humble backgrounds find themselves working with other levels of British society, leading to an enhanced understanding of how our unique British system works. They see themselves among the keepers of the kingdom, supporting this country's structure of government through the democracy of an elected parliament with the continuance and stability of a crowned Head of State.

PROUD TO SERVE
PROUD TO UPHOLD TRADITION
PROUD OF THEIR RIVER ORIGINS

NOTABLE EVENTS FOR HM BARGEMASTERS AND ROYAL WATERMEN

1215	First written evidence. King John's barge at Runnymede for Magna Carta.
1264	Queen Eleanor attacked at London Bridge.
1272	Edward I returned from his four-year crusade to great river celebrations.
1290	Edward II's Royal Watermen rescued the King from an attack on the River Fleet.
1514	Henry VIII's first Act of Parliament to control Thames watermen.
1555	Another Act to form a Watermen's Guild and one-year apprenticeships.
1558	Elizabeth I's Grant of Arms to the Watermen's Guild.
1580–83	John Taylor, Royal Waterman to a Queen, two Kings and a dictator.
1581	Royal Watermen wounded in Royal Barge by gunshot.
1665	The Great Plague. Watermen rowed corpses down river to plague pits.
1666	The Great Fire. Watermen rowed people out of the City from the fire.
1692	William III and Mary II built a hospital at Greenwich for seamen.
1714	George I, Doggett's Coat and Badge Race. Oldest annual sporting event.
1738	Capture of Spanish fleet at Port of Bella. Crews included many Watermen.
1770	Impressment; 110 Watermen broke free from ships moored at Grays in Essex.
1797	Nelson's coxswain, Waterman Sam Shillingford, killed at Battle of Tenerife.
1805	After the Battle of Trafalgar, Nelson's body was rowed in State to Westminster.

1807	Watermen volunteered to sail home captured Danish fleet: 375 men manned thirty-three ships.
1821	William IV opened the New London Bridge. Dramatic change to tidal regime.
1841	Fire at Tower of London. Keeper of the Tower rescued the Crown Jewels.
1858	The Great Stink. Loss of Lord Mayor's Show and many Royal river duties.
1864	Joseph Bazalgette embankment. The river now much narrower for navigation.
1894	Tower Bridge built. Upper and Lower Pool created increased Port of London activity.
1927	HM Bargemaster Bert Barry, Professional World Champion Sculler.
1940	Boats sailed from the Thames to rescue 300,000 soldiers from Dunkirk.
1940	7 September, heaviest air raid on London Docks. River vessels ablaze.
1941	Watermen volunteered for Millionaires' Navy, for dummy invasion fleet.
1952	Elizabeth II crowned. Retinue of twenty-four Watermen and Bargemaster.
1964	Watermen allowed to race as amateurs. Many now compete at Henley.
1965	Funeral of Sir Winston Churchill. Royal Watermen in attendance.
1968 & 1972	HM Bargemaster K. Dwan rowed in two Olympic Games.
1973	The Queen opens New London Bridge. Royal Barge in attendance.
1973	The Queen's Silver Jubilee. The Queen on river attended by her Watermen.
2001	Golden Jubilee. Watermen photographed with Her Majesty in Throne Room.
2010	HM Waterman Robert Prentice rowed in two Cross Atlantic Races.
2012	The Queen's Diamond Jubilee pageant. New State Row-Barge *Gloriana* built
2015	Royal Watermen's 800th anniversary. Among longest-serving in Royal household.

GLOSSARY

Almshouse:	Home for the support of the old, poor and decayed.
Bargemaster:	Captain in charge of a ceremonial rowing barge.
Beadle:	Guild Inspector; early form of policeman.
Capstan:	A hand-powered lifting device.
Careen:	To purposely list a ship over to enable work on its hull.
City Fathers:	Lord Major and City Council.
Disembark:	To leave a vessel.
Draw Dock:	A tidal beach used for boat repair.
Embark:	To come on board a vessel.
Ebb:	The tide draining out from land to the sea.
Farthing:	¼ of an old penny (12 pennies to one shilling).
Flood:	The tidal flow running in from the sea.
Frost Fair:	Frozen river, the iced area used for merry-making.
Gunwale:	Top edge of the side planking of a boat or ship.
Guinea:	A coin worth one pound and a shilling.
Knave:	A person with a bad or naughty reputation.
The Livery:	The Trading Guilds of the City of London.
Lash-down:	An arrangement of rope fastenings.
Landing Stairs:	A place where wherries would be waiting for passengers.
Livery Hall:	Grand building for the business of a Trading Guild.
Livery barge:	Large vessel for entertaining the Guild's members.
Licence Plate:	Waterman's licence number, worn on the upper left arm.
Mooring Post:	Upright timber for tying a boat's catch-line onto.
Old London Bridge:	Nineteen arches. Acted as a weir or dam on the ebb tide.
Oars!:	A call for summoning a wherry (water taxi).
Playhouse:	An early theatre.
Press Gang:	Naval personnel, taking men for service aboard fighting ships.

Port and Starboard:	The left and right-hand side of a vessel.
Penny:	$\frac{1}{12}$ of a Shilling (20 shillings to one pound).
Raddan Style:	Wherry rowed by two men for extra speed.
Royal Waterman:	Chosen man appointed to row the Royal Barge.
Rulers:	Overall government of the Watermen.
Rowing Wager:	A professional rowing race between Watermen.
Samson Post:	The main mooring bollard sited at the bow of a vessel.
Shallop:	Fast oared vessel for river passenger transport.
Tilt:	A small cabin or enclosed area for the protection of passengers.
Tow Rag:	An outcast of the City, employed to pull cargo barges upstream.
Watergate:	A river entrance to a grand house.
Wherry:	Small one-man operated oared vessel for transporting fare-paying passengers.
Wherryman:	Licensed Waterman trained and licensed via the Watermen's Guild.
Whiffler:	Lookout stationed at the bow of a nobleman's barge.

RESEARCH SOURCES

Primary Sources

Historic Manuscripts Commission.

House of Commons Journals.

House of Lords Journals.

Letters of John Taylor.

National Archives:
  Appointment Books
  Calendars State Papers
  Calendar of Treasury Books and Treasury Papers
  King's Warrant Book
  Letters and Papers, Foreign and Domestic
  Privy Purse Accounts
  Treasury Papers
  Treasury Warrants
  Wardrobe Accounts
  Warrants of the Council of State

Nichols, J.G. (ed.), *The Diary of Henry Machin, Citizen and Merchant Taylor of London 1550–1563* (additional notes to the text).

Parliament Rolls of Medieval England, ed. Chris Given-Wilson, Paul Brand, Seymour Phillips, Mark Ormrod, Geoffrey Martin, Anne Curry and Rosemary Horrox (Woodbridge, 2005), British History Online www.british-history.ac.uk/no-series/parliament-rolls-medieval [accessed 22 May 2019].

Regulations for the Gentlemen Ushers in the Reign of Charles II (1787).

The Royal Collections Trust.

Secondary Sources

Beale, Philip, *England's Mail* (2005).

Belle Assemblée; or, *Court and Fashionable Magazine,* Vol. XIV (1831).

Birch, G.H., *London on the Thames* (1903).

Bucholz, R.O., *The Augustan Court* (1993).

Byerly, Benjamin F. and Catherine Ridder (eds), *Records of the Wardrobe and Household* (1977).

Campbell, John Lord, *The Lives of the Lord Chancellors & Keepers of the Great Seal* (1848).

Campbell, Williams (ed.), *Materials for a History of the Reign of Henry VII* (1877).

Cavell, Emma, *The Herald's Memoir 1486–1490* (2019).

Cole, Mary Hill, *The Portable Queen: Elizabeth I and the Politics of Ceremony* (1998).

Devon, Frederick, *Issues of the Exchequer during the Reign of James I* (1836).

Dodd, Christopher, *Unto the Tideway Born* (2015).

'Dress to be Worn at Court', issued by the Lord Chamberlain.

Edwards, Peter, *The Horse Trade of Tudor and Stuart England* (1988).

Folger Shakespeare Library Manuscripts.

Forster, J., *Eminent British Statesmen: Oliver Cromwell* (1839).

Fraser, Antonia, *King Charles II* (1979).

Given-Wilson, Chris, Kettle, Ann and Scales, Len (eds), *War, Government and Aristocracy in the British Isles 1150–1500* (2008).

Gregory, William, *Chronicle of London* (1876).

Guy, John, notes on The Marian Court and Tudor Policy Making.

Hayward, Maria (ed.), *The Great Wardrobe Accounts of Henry VII and Henry VIII* (2012).

Hillam, J., *Ancient Monuments Laboratory Report 73/97*.

Hilton, Lisa, *Elizabeth, Renaissance Prince* (2014).

Holmes, Martin and Sitwell, Major General H.D.W., *English Regalia* (1972).

Hopkins, J. Castell, *The Life of King Edward VII* (1902).

Humpherus, Henry, *History of the Origin and Progress of the Company of Watermen and Lightermen of the River Thames* (1992).

Johnstone-Bryden, Richard, *River Pageants of the Past*.

Jonas, Michael K. and Underwood, Malcolm, *The King's Mother: Lady Margaret Beaufort, Countess of Richmond and Derby* (1992).

Kuhns, Matt, *Cotton's Library: The Many Perils of Preserving History* (2014).

Lega-Weekes, Ethel, *The King's Old Barge House* (c.1900).

Lewis, Matthew, *Henry III: The Son of Magna Carta* (2016).

'Mary II's Officers and Servants', online database.

Mortimer, Ian, *1415: Henry V's Year of Glory* (1967).

Mortimer, Ian, *The Time Traveller's Guide to Elizabethan England* (2013).

Nicolas, Sir Nicholas Harris, *The Privy Purse Expenses of Elizabeth of York: Wardrobe Accounts* (1830).

Nicholls, John, *Progresses and Public Processions of Queen Elizabeth* (1823).

Nichols, John Gough, *London Pageants* (1831).

Norton, Peter, *State Barges* (1972).

O'Riordan, Christopher, *The Thames Watermen in the Century of Revolution* (1992).

Palmer, Alan and Veronica, *The Chronology of British History* (1992).

Palmer, Kenneth Nicholls, *Ceremonial Barges on the River Thames* (1997).

Parker, Michael St John, *Royal River* (1989).

Pearce, Dominic, *Henrietta Maria* (2015).

Pearce, Robert R., *A History of the Inns of Court and Chancery* (1848).

Phelps, Maurice, *The Phelps Dynasty* (2012).

Planche, J.P., *Regal Records Or a Chronicle of the Coronations of the Queens Regnand of England* (1838).

Richardson, John, *Annals of London: Year by Year* (2000).

Society of Antiquaries, *Archaeological: Or Miscellaneous Tracts Relating to Antiquity* (1786).

Starkey, David, *Royal Ritual and the River* (2012).

Starkey, David, *Six Wives: The Queens of Henry VIII* (2004).

Strong, Roy, *Coronation* (2005).

Strype's Memorials (c.1800).

Temple, John, *The History of the Origin and Progress of the Company of Watermen and Lightermen* (2008).

The Alleynian, Issue 636.

The Gentleman's Magazine.

Thornbury, Walter, *Old and New London,* Vol. 3 (London, 1878), British History Online www.british-history.ac.uk/old-new-london/vol3 [accessed 22 May 2019].

Thurley, Simon, *Royal Palaces of Tudor England* (1993).

Thurley, Simon, 'The Vanishing Architecture of the River Thames', *Royal River: Power Pageantry and the Thames* (2012).

Vale, Malcolm, *Princely Court: Medieval Courts and Culture, North West Europe* (2001).

Walpole, Horace, *Anecdotes of Painting in England* (1762).

Warner, Kathryn, *Edward II The Unconventional King* (2008).

Weir, Alison, *Henry VIII: King and Court* (2002).

Woodward, Jennifer, *The Theatre of Death* (1997).

Wriothesley, Charles, *Chronicle of England* (1877).

Wylie, James Hamilton, *Henry The Fifth* (1914).

NOTES

Chapter I
1 *Henry III: The Son of Magna Carta*, by Mathew Lewis.

Chapter II
1 *The Royal Palaces of Tudor England*, by Simon Thurley.
2 *The Six Wives of Henry VIII*, by Alison Weir.
3 *Six Wives: The Queens of Henry VIII*, by David Starkey.
4 *Unto the Tideway Born*, by Christopher Dodd.
5 *History of the Origin and Progress of the Company of Watermen and Lightermen of the River Thames*, by Henry Humpherus.
6 Calendar of State Papers of Edward, Mary and Elizabeth 1547–80.
7 *Elizabeth, Renaissance Prince*, by Lisa Hilton.
8 *A History of the Inns of Court and Chancery*, by Robert Pearce.
9 *King Charles II*, by Antonia Fraser.
10 *Letters of John Taylor.*
11 National Archives E101/541/11.
12 *The Home Counties Magazine.*
13 *London on Thames*, by G.H. Birch.
14 *The Courant.*
15 *History of the Watermen's Company*, by Henry Humpherus.
16 *History of the Watermen's Company*, by Henry Humpherus.
17 *Belle Assemblee; or Court and Fashionable Magazine* (1831).
18 *Old and New London*, by T. Cadell.
19 *The Life of King Edward VIII*, by J. Castell Hopkins.
20 *History of the Origin and Progress of the Company of Watermen and Lightermen of the River Thames*, by Jon Temple.
21 *The Times* (1937).
22 *History of the Watermen's Company*, by Henry Humpherus.
23 *The Lives of the Lord Chancellors and Keepers of the Great Seal*, by John Lord Campbell.
24 *History of the Watermen's Company*, by Henry Humpherus.
25 National Archives CSP Warrants of Protector and Council.
26 *History of the Watermen's Company*, by Henry Humpherus.
27 *History of the Watermen's Company*, by Henry Humpherus.
28 National Archives SP/46/1/fo2 London Pageants.
29 *History of the Watermen's Company*, by Henry Humpherus.
30 *The Herald's Memoir 1486–90*, by Emma Cavell.
31 *Henry VIII: King and Court*, by Alison Weir.

32 National Archives SP46/1/fo2.

33 *Regal Records Or a Chronicle of the Coronations of the Queens Regnand of England*, by J.P. Planche.

34 *Elizabeth: Renaissance Prince*, by Lisa Hilton.

35 National Archives E36/214.

36 *Six Wives – The Queens of Henry VIII*, by David Starkey.

37 House of Lords Library Note.

38 House of Lords Library Note.

39 House of Lords Library Note.

40 Calendar of Treasury Books 1714.

41 Calendar of Treasury Papers 1716.

42 *Royal Ritual and the River*, by David Starkey.

43 *Royal Ritual and the River*, by David Starkey.

44 *Henrietta Maria*, by Dominic Pearce.

45 *History of the Watermen and Lightermen*, by Jon Temple.

46 *History of the Watermen's Company*, by Henry Humpherus.

47 *History of the Watermen's Company*, by Henry Humpherus.

48 *The Theatre of Death*, by Jennifer Woodward.

49 Privy Purse Expenses of Henry VIII.

50 Close Rolls 1389–1392.

51 Calendar of Treasury Books.

52 King's Warrant Book.

Chapter III

1 Records of the Wardrobe & Household of Edward I.

2 Patent Roll 10 Henry IV.

3 *1415: Henry V's Year of Glory*, by Ian Mortimer.

4 Calendar of State Papers Edward IV.

5 *Letters and Papers of the Reign of Henry VIII*, John Brewer (ed.).

6 *Letters & Papers Henry VIII*, John Brewer (ed.).

7 *Letters & Papers Henry VIII*, John Brewer (ed.).

8 *Letters & Papers Henry VIII*, John Brewer (ed.).

9 Treasurer of the Chamberlain's Accounts 1531–1532.

10 *Chronicle of England*, by Charles Wriothesley.

11 Letters & Papers Foreign and Domestic 1531/2.

12 Privy Purse Expenses of Henry VIII.

13 National Archives SP/1/fo2.

14 Calendar of Patent Rolls.

15 Calendar of Patent Rolls.

16 Calendar of Patent Rolls of Philip & Mary.

17 National Archives C3/98/57.

18 National Archives LC2/4/4.

19 Calendar of State Papers, Don James I.

20 Calendar of State Papers, James I.

21 National Archives C3/98/57.

22 National Archives LC2/4/4.

23 Parliamentary Papers.

24 House of Lords Journal 1660.

25 Calendar of Treasury Books 1660–1.

26 Archaelogica: Or Miscellaneous Tracts relating to Antiquity.

27 Folger Shakespeare Library Manuscripts.

28 Calendar of State Papers.

29 National Archives.

30 PRO – SP16/135.

31 Proceedings of the Committee of both houses at Derby House on 14 July 1648.

32 CSP Dom – Letters & Papers relating to the Navy 1655–1656.

33 Warrants of the Council of State 1659/60.

34 National Archives PROB11/301/139.

35 House of Commons Journal May 1660.

36 Calendar of Treasury Books 1661.

37 Calendar of Treasury Books 1666.

38 National Archives PROB 11/387.

39 National Archives – Treasury Books.

40 National Archives – Treasury Books.

41 Calendar of Treasury Books.

42 Calendar of Treasury Books 1711.

43 Historic Manuscripts Commission.

44 Calendar of Treasury Books 1717.

45 *The Gentlemen's Magazine.*

46 National Archives LC3/58.

47 *The Monthly Magazine*, 1796.

48 National Archives LC3/68.

49 The Metropolitan 1897.

Chapter VI

1 Calendar of Patent Rolls.

2 National Archives LC3/56.

3 National Archives LC3/58.

4 Wardrobe Accounts of Edward IV.

5 National Archives LC2/9.

6 National Archives LC2/18.

7 The Diary of Henry Machin, Citizen & Merchant Taylor of London 1550–1563.

8 Calendar of Treasury Books 1685–1689.

9 National Archives LC3/57.

10 Calendar of Treasury Books 1713.

11 Calendar of Treasury Books 1714.

12 Calendar of Treasury Books 1717.

13 Calendar of Treasury Books 1729.

14 'Dress to be Worn at Court' – issued by the Lord Chamberlain.

15 Calendar of State Papers Dom: Interregnum.

16 Calendar of Treasury Books 1689–92.

17 Calendar of Treasury Books 1702.

18 Treasury Warrants 1708.

19 Calendar of Treasury Books 1708.

20 Warrants not relating to money.

21 Warrant Books 1715.

22 Warrant Books 1715.

23 Treasury Books.

24 Treasury Papers.

25 *London on Thames*, by G.H. Birch.

26 *Chronicle of London*, by William Gregory.

Chapter VII

1 Calendar of Treasury Books 1685–1689.

Chapter VIII

1 National Archives E317/Surrey/49.

2 Calendar of Treasury Books 1693–1696.

3 Calendar of Treasury Papers.

4 Calendar of Books 1716.

5 Treasury Warrants.

6 National Archives T1/421.

Chapter IX

1 *Henry VIII: King and Court*, by Alison Weir.

2 The Marian Court & Tudor Policy Making.

3 *History of the Watermen's Company*, by Henry Humpherus.

4 *The Alleynian*, Special Issue.

5 *Issues of the Exchequer during the reign of King James I*, by Frederick Devon.

6 National Archives C66/1666.

7 *Issues of the Exchequer during the reign of King James I*, by Frederick Devon.

8 House of Commons Journal Vol. 5.

9 House of Lords Journal 1660.

10 Warrant Books 1715.

11 Calendar of Treasury Books 1717.

12 *State Barges*, by Peter Norton.

13 *Unto the Tideway Born*, by Christopher Dodd.

14 National Archives.

Chapter X

1 'The Vanishing Architecture of the River Thames', by Simon Thurley.

2 Ancient Monuments Laboratory Report 73/97.

3 'The Vanishing Architecture of the River Thames', by Simon Thurley.

ABOUT THE AUTHORS

BERYL PENDLEY LL.B.
Barrister – Inner Temple (Called 1994)
College of Arms – 10 years
Assistant and Genealogist to Henry Paston-Bedingfeld when he was Rouge
Croix Pursuivant and then York Herald
College of Arms – appointed by the College as Clerk of the Ordinaries
Principal of Reger Research UK
Vice-President Conservative Foreign & Commonwealth Council – 15 years
(retired)
Trustee Rowland Hill Fund – 20-plus years (retired)
Member First Aid Nursing Yeomanry 20-plus years

ROBERT G. CROUCH MVO
1953 Apprenticed Thames waterman
1958 Doggett's Coat & Badge winner
1958 National Service, RN, two years
1960, '61, '62 Raced at Henley Regattas
1969 MD, Catamaran Cruises Ltd
1980 Appointed Royal Waterman
1987 Master of Watermen's Co.
1988 Appointed HM Bargemaster
1989 MD Thames Line Riverbus Co.
2001 Awarded MVO by HM Queen
2002 Clerk to Watermen's Guild
2005 Professional model-making
2006 Writing first novel, *The Coat of Doggett*
2008 Various. Traditional Rowing and Coxing instructional booklets
2015 Presentation book, for Royal Watermen, gift to HM Queen
2016 Tour guide for Watermen's Hall